I AM DAVID

A Pastor's Fall Into Grace

MICKEY BELL

Publisher: Absolute Author Publishing House

Editor: Dr. Melissa Caudle

LIBRARY OF CONGRESS CATALOGUE IN-PUBLICATION-DATA

I Am David/Mickey Bell

p. cm.

Paperback ISBN: 978-1-64953-131-5

eBook ISBN: 978-1-64953-063-9

1. Spiritual   2. Religious 3. Self-help

Printed in the United States of America

www.TheMickeyBell.com

FOREWORD

Rev. Mickey Bell has been forthright and very transparent in the writing of his journey and calling in life. Not everyone can be as transparent as Mickey in revealing how unfortunate decisions and wrong decisions can be costly to our spiritual lives.

His journey was tumultuous, broken, and filled with desperation. There was a constant and daily fear of who was going to find out the moral failure. What would be the church's response if the information was made public? Would the church's response be one of compassion and restoration or judgment?

I was introduced to Bro. Mickey by one of his staff members in 2014. During that initial introduction and acquaintance by telephone, a process of restoration was initiated. A process of church discipline was initiated for the purpose of restoration. God was not through with Bro. Mickey, but he had a process to go through so God could use him again.

Three individuals were trained in church discipline to work with Bro. Mickey. The journey was one of approximately eight months. Bro. Mickey was not permitted to do ministry without the restoration team's approval. The journey was challenging, but the ministry team did not give up on Bro. Mickey. Neither did Bro. Mickey.

Church Discipline is a biblical process for the purpose of restoration. It is sad that some churches treat church discipline as excommunication instead of restoration. In the Beltic Confession of 1567, it described a true New Testament Church as one that practiced the observance of baptism and the Lord's Supper. It also included the practice of church discipline. Churches today find themselves as stagnant or declining instead of being spiritually healthy due to unresolved sinful issues of the past.

Bro. Mickey was restored unconditionally to ministry. God has renewed His calling on Bro. Mickey's life. He is a special blessing to his family, his church, and his ministry, and his community.

As God did this for Bro. Mickey, He will also do this for you. Never forget that God loves you so much that the least He can give to you is His best!!!

Dr. Barry F. Cosper
Associational Missionary
Bessemer Baptist Association
Bessemer, AL 35022

REFERENCES

"What a story, read and listen as the man of scriptures becomes the man in the mirror. Be blessed as you read an encouraging finish to a challenging story."

Pastor Johnny Hunt
First Baptist Church
Woodstock, Ga.

"Transparency. Some talk about it and some do it. Mickey Bell is in the latter category. In I Am David you'll find an unvarnished unpacking of a man and leader's life-struggles. It will help you and other men you know."

Sam Chand
Leadership Consultant and author of Leadership Pain

"Pastor Mickey hit the ball out of the park with his latest book, "I Am David!" I began reading it one evening and could not put it down. His brutal honesty and transparency about personal struggles and storms are both refreshing and challenging. If you are tired of living with discouragement and defeat and desire freedom ... real freedom ... God's freedom ... do yourself a favor and read, I Am David!"

Dr. Kevin J. Hamm
Senior Pastor Gardendale First Baptist Church

"No matter if you are a pastor, worship leader or musician, the fact is we are all subject to the struggles that Pastor Mickey had to deal with. I am thankful for a man who is bold enough to be so transparent in efforts to helping other people. "I Am David" is a book that that will change every life that takes time to read it."

Mark Lee from Third Day,
author of Hurt Road: The Music, the Memories, and the Miles Between

CHAPTER 1
The Worst Monday Ever

Who are you? No, not the person you want to be or the person you used to be, but who are you now? No, not who others think you are, but I'm talking about the real you. The part of you that no one ever sees. The part of you that you hope no one ever sees. The person you look at every morning when you look in the mirror.

Now that you are staring that person in the face, how do you feel about who you really are? Are you okay with that person? Are you okay with the life you are living?

If you could change that person, what would you want to change? Are there decisions you have made in your past that you wish you could undo? I am sure there are things you have said that you wish you could go back and unsay. There are moments in your life that you wish you could get a do-over. But you can't.

So now you are forced to live with the person that you see every morning in the mirror. And if you are like me, you don't particularly care for the reflection that is coming back at you. While others see the success you are, you see the sinner that you are. While others see all the good you have done, you know about all the bad you have done.

While others may want to be you, you wish you could live in the skin of someone else.

I AM DAVID!

Mickey Bell

I know full well how you feel because . . . I AM DAVID!

It was Monday morning. This is the day every pastor wants to quit or retire to another occupation (you will understand if you are a pastor). I had just given everything I had within me the day before during our Sunday service.

The church was growing. Exciting things were happening. But I wasn't ready for what was about to take place. Behind the scenes, something was stirring. A coup was being created without my knowledge.

Reporting for my office duties, I was met at the door by two of the elders who had a look on their faces I had never seen before. The next few moments would be the toughest moments of my life.

The only way I can describe this moment of what I was feeling - *Devastated! Heartbroken! Wretched! Miserable!*

I felt as though someone had just punched me in the gut, and for days, I could not breathe without hurting. The elders of the church that called me pastor for four years just informed me that I was relieved of my duties. Were they looking for something to get rid of me? Many seem to think so.

I don't know what I did to hurt them. I am still not sure what caused them to have a change of heart about me and my services. All I know is it only takes a few to start looking, but the problem was, I had something for them to find.

There was something in the closet of my past that I had kept hidden for about four years. I wasn't ready for it to become public. In fact, I had it so tucked away in my past that I thought it would never make an appearance. I surely wasn't ready for it to be used against me. But that skeleton I had put away and hid for years was making a comeback, and this time, with a vengeance.

I had to tell my wife and my little girl that in a matter of ten minutes, I was without a job, an income, and a house. In a matter of moments, my family was homeless, and there was nothing I could do to stop it or even help it. I didn't know if I was going to be divorced or found dead somewhere off the side of the road. I felt as though all the church people hated me, and I didn't blame them because I hated myself. Family members were hurt; so-called friends were nowhere to be found. All of a sudden, I went from being the guy everyone wanted to share life with to the guy who everyone wanted to avoid.

My thoughts were all over the place. I wanted to cry, and I did, a lot! I wanted to scream, and I did . . . a lot! I wanted to run, and I almost did . . . many times. But something inside—or should I say someone inside of me kept me sane, in an insane state of mind. Not because of how I might have been done wrong but because the wrong that was done was all my fault. It was me!

It was my fault that I was, in that moment, a huge failure. It was my fault that for the next twenty-four hours I didn't know if I would ever see my family again. It was because of my decisions I had not thought of a future that was enticing enough to keep me alive. There was nothing anyone could say or do that could pull me out of this.

Have you been there? I mean come on; I am the pastor of a growing church. We are not supposed to have issues. We are sup- posed to be pristine and polished with everything put together. We are not to show ourselves as being weak or messed up.

I AM DAVID!

Mickey Bell

Even if you don't have it all together, you are to present yourself

as almost perfect. And even though people will say, "No one is perfect except Christ," the church really expected you to be. I was making decisions that was even terrifying me.

But out of all the people who were hearing about my transgressions, I was the last person that was surprised. These people may have only known me for a short period of time, but I have had to live with these issues all my life. People were forced to hear so many versions of a story in which some were true, but not all. So, decisions were being made on the person I really was.

Once you hear my life story, you might better understand yourself. It doesn't excuse it, by no means, but it does put perspective on how we are all controlled by forces that we don't realize. How decisions made for us will also be used against us if not dealt with properly.

All I wanted to do was simply stay in the bed and hide under my pillows. I wanted to change my name and move to a deserted island where no one would know who I was. While Christians were trying to destroy me, I was just trying to stay alive. They did everything they could do to keep me from bouncing back from this. They not only wanted me to leave their church, they didn't want me to live in the community. Any church we visited; they made a call. Any landlord we tried to rent from, they made a visit.

I had hurt them. I had let them down. I had presented to them great promises of a bright future to only end up being a huge letdown. I know we all make mistakes, but I don't know if everyone has made a mistake this big. In that moment of despair and confusion, I felt all alone. The church that once surrounded me with love was now surrounding to harass me. Those that would "amen" during the message I preached on

offering forgiveness to others changed their minds when it was the pastor that needed forgiveness.

What do you do when it's the pastor that needs the help? Why can't a pastor admit he has done wrong?

Who is supposed to sit and listen to the pastor when he has demons to deal with?

For twenty-four hours, my life came to a screeching halt, and for once in my life, I felt all alone, which, as you will see later, was the biggest fear of my life. Sure, there were a few people around me, but I was so numb to the situation. I could see them standing around, but I couldn't feel their presence at all around me.

They were simply images of bodies I wished I could switch with, but through my sight of tears and heartache, it was a bad dream that never woke me up.

Everywhere I went, I could feel the people talking behind my back. I couldn't go anywhere without running into people that knew what I did. They seemed to be everywhere. People who called on me when they were dealing with sins of their own. People who reached out to me when they needed to be pulled out of the grips of Satan himself. There was plenty of redemption for them, just not for the pastor.

Even though I had heard of other church leaders doing what I had done, I still felt as though I was all alone. There were people in the church who had done what I did, but it was so long ago for them, they were more interested in running as far away from me as they could get instead of sticking around to help. My wife was there, but she really didn't want to be. My daughter was there, but she was so young she didn't fully comprehend what was going on. All she knew was everyone hated her and her

mom and dad, and she didn't know why.

And I am not sure what my little girl did to draw the hate that was being thrown at her. All I could figure out was they were harassing her to get back at me. Should I expect any less? This is a church we are talking about. Now I am dealing with anger because of how they are treating two innocent lives who did nothing to hurt them.

I wanted to get vengeance. I wanted people to hurt like I was hurting. I wanted to expose all the secrets I knew on those who were hurting me. But I kept silent.

So, there I am. A poor excuse for a man, a father, much less a pastor. I can understand why so many would hate me. When it comes to ignoring me in public places, I can see why they would choose to walk out of their way to avoid me. Trust me, I didn't want to be in my skin, much less have to communicate with me either.

I know I let a lot of people down. I let my family down . . .

I let myself down.

With more than seven billion people in this world, I was all alone.

Who in this world would know how I feel? Is there anyone who could relate to the struggle I now have before me? Is there anyone who can hear me in my pain even though I don't have the strength to scream for help?

I was hoping to run to anyone that could relate. I was looking for others who would know the pain I was feeling. Heck, I just wanted a shoulder to cry on without judgment or regret—

someone who wouldn't judge me but would actually love me.

It was though I suddenly heard someone calling out my name. It was odd because I had never met this person even though I seemed to know a lot about him. I don't just mean I knew of him, but I knew intimate details about his life. In fact, a lot of people knew it. It wasn't like it was kept a big secret. They even wrote a book and included this guy's life in it.

From the moment I was in Sunday school, I have heard about this man. We praised him for the good he did and learned from the mistakes he committed. I was introduced to him when he was just a shepherd boy doing chores out in a field. I heard the heroic stories of when he killed a lion and a bear. And then the day he picked up a stone and used his sling shot to kill a giant. Are you kidding me? He was more like a hero to men than just a biblical character. I loved learning about him.

While I couldn't see him, I could feel him. While I couldn't see him, I could sense him calling me to come closer to him as though he wanted to share something with me. For the next few years, I sat down with this guy named David, who spoke into my life.

It was though he knew exactly what I was going through. He would describe his feelings, and it would be as though he was describing me. He could touch a sensitive nerve for me when he was actually talking about himself. Not only did he teach me about pain, but he also showed me how to pray. When I couldn't find the words to say, I noticed he had already said them for me. He was able to describe how I was feeling when going before Almighty God.

I mean, what do you say when you have to face God with something like this? I was leading one of his churches. It was my voice he was using to deliver his messages each week. I need help in

approaching this holy God with my unholy self.

I wasn't expecting God to be so loving. I wasn't anticipating him to be so forgiving. I really thought he would be like the people who were in my life. I thought for sure God would just throw me away. I wouldn't even blame Him if he sent me off and forgot about me, but He didn't. Since the church is supposed to be a representation of Him, I was expecting to be shunned, hated, and forced out.

The words "I'm sorry" and "Forgive me" just didn't seem powerful enough to pull me out of this situation. Nothing I could say made sense, and nothing I could do would make up for it. I anticipate someone has picked up this book and you feel as though I have just described to you. You may not be a pastor, but you are an individual who has made a bad decision; a decision that is affecting you and your family.

But then again, you may be a pastor. One who was called to lead, and you have been secretly dealing with demons that up until now you were afraid to acknowledge. Sharing your secrets would be ministry suicide. In fact, you may be shaking while holding this book in your hands, simply afraid of people finding out who you really are when you are not on stage.

Just breathe.

I am not here to expose you, but to love you. I am not here to knock you but lift you up. I am going to share the story of this man in the Bible who taught me what it's like to knock yourself down with decisions and get back up again. He has been where you are right now.

He taught me what it was like to feel so rejected and scared that you wanted to hide out in a cave, praying for your own life. By

the words of his testimony that was recorded more than two thousand years ago, I came to the realization that while people might call me by my given name, I stand here today to admit to you that …I am David.

CHAPTER 2
Meet My New Friend

It was as though a new kid had just moved into town. As I spent time with him, I started learning things about him that caused me to want to learn even more.

My new friend David started telling me stories of growing up in a small area outside of Bethlehem. I didn't understand why he wanted me to know all this information because I didn't feel like it had anything to do with me or my current situation. He was a shepherd boy who had the chore of tending to sheep. I didn't even have a dog growing up. But as he continued to speak, I continued to listen. David would eventually become a king, and very few people could even compare to that status. But it wasn't his place in the palace that had my attention; it was the problems in his personal life that had me glued to his story.

I was not listening to David through my thoughts as a pastor. I wasn't trying to find three points and a great illustration to share with others. In fact, I had spent so much time preaching about him. I was wondering what more this guy was going to share with me that I didn't already know. But with the prompting of the Holy Spirit, I continued to listen as I took a journey with my new friend back to the day where he felt a major disappointment. It should have been the most exciting day of his life, and it was, even for Israel, but that wasn't the case for David.

King Saul was one who would listen and obey God while he was climbing the ladder of success, but once he got into power, the

king did what a lot of people will do. He forgot who got him

there. And just like so many others, Saul didn't feel the need to contact God any longer. All his decisions were based on how it benefited him as king. It was no longer based on what God wanted; it was all based on what pleased the king.

So, decision after decision, King Saul continued to move further and further away from God and His guidance. No longer praying, just playing. No longer seeking God, but now just seeking approval from man. This is a good place to take notes. The Almighty will only let you go so far, and once you have crossed his line; you are finished. Well, Saul did just that. He crossed God's line, and now Saul was about to be replaced. But with who?

Who would even be remotely qualified to take over? Saul didn't have anyone in the shadows that he was mentoring to take over. I can't even believe I said that with a straight face. His pride wouldn't allow him to call on God. You think he was going to turn over his power to someone else? His ego had him staying in power for much longer. So, the search was on. God began searching the world to find a valid replacement. Someone who would listen to the commands of God. Someone who in spite of his successful moments, he would still honor and offer praise to the actual source of his victories. Someone who . . . well . . . someone who had a heart for God.

And that is where David starts telling me his story.

He told me how a prophet came to his house, but he didn't know anything about his arrival or why he was even there. David said he was just out in the field doing what he was supposed do because even back then, boys had to do chores. His job was to care for the sheep. This was not a glamorous job and especially not one that was sought after. He would lead the sheep to a

stream so they could stay hydrated. He would constantly look for green grass to lead his fold when their current place of food became bare. He was also having to watch out for predators who would try to work themselves into the group, wanting to bring harm or even kill his sheep. So, he was always on guard, looking, expecting, and anticipating when the enemy would be drawing near.

David was always on guard. He was a good shepherd who knew how to take care of his sheep. But this wasn't his favorite job to do. As a young boy, you don't hope and dream that one day you can grow worship service. While the animals were roaming, David was focusing on his music while also keeping an eye out on his responsibility. Hour after hour began to pass, and the day was about halfway to completion when he noticed something happening.

He was far enough away that he couldn't really see, but while in the field, he heard a noise taking place up near the home place. It was the sound of commotion that was heard when a visitor was coming on to the property. The animals around the house served as a doorbell to alert the family that someone who wasn't supposed to be there was there.

David started working his way into position to try and figure out who was responsible for all the commotion. As he made his way into sight of the house, he could see they had a visitor. He didn't recognize the man who was talking to his dad, so David just continued his worship service while watching over his sheep.

He thought something was a little strange, when Jesse, his

19

father, started yelling for all the boys to come to the house. Well, everyone except David. His dad just started calling the boys by their name, and when he got to David's name, there was silence. For some reason, Jesse didn't think David needed to be included.

I could hear it in David's voice. The feeling of being left out while his brothers got to meet the guest of the house. Why would his dad call everyone in, but him? Was he not a part of this family too?

Here's what David said to me about that day . . .

"So, I remained in the field just minding my own business. It wasn't until I got brought into the house that I fully realized what had just happened. You see, the prophet Samuel was sent to our house by the Lord to anoint the next king of Israel. I thought that was pretty cool until it hit me that my dad didn't bring me in on the first go-around. I noticed they were all getting paraded in front of this man even though I didn't know at the moment why. Then I started wondering to myself if the prophet had the right house. I mean, one of my brothers becoming king. Yeah right. But then it hit me. While I was standing there, watching all my brothers, I kept wondering why my dad would just forget about me and leave me out in the field, especially when it's something as major as one of us boys becoming a king. I would have loved to have been there when this major announcement was made. Am I not important enough to be included? Is that what my dad thinks about me? Wow! My dad forgot about me."

In that moment of hearing David's story, I felt a knot come up in my throat because I knew exactly how my friend felt. It's a part of my testimony I have been sharing since I was sixteen years old. It wasn't something I was ever ashamed to tell, so I didn't think it had any type of hold on me. I never would have imagined it would affect me like it did much later in my life. In fact, it effected every day of my life, but I was unaware of its motives.

I remember it like it happened yesterday. After coming home from church on a Sunday afternoon, Mom was finishing up a

home cooked lunch, which she provided every Sunday. We sat down as a family as we always did—Dad, Mom, my brother, my three sisters, and me. After we had finished our lunch, I suspected that our normal routine would take place. Dad would go to his chair for an afternoon nap, and I would go to my room to listen to music. But something different was happening on this particular day.

I thought something was up when my dad asked me if I wanted to go riding with him on his motorcycle. I was running through my mind if I had done something wrong. I was trying to figure out what my dad needed with me. This was a bit unusual, and why me? Why not Paul, Melody, Andrea, or Sisa? But for some reason, Dad just wanted me to make this trip with him. We left our house in Section, and he took the back roads behind Hodge Church. We ended up on the backside of Taco Bet, which was the local flea market on Sundays. Right across from Tutor's Garage was an opening that overlooked the Tennessee River. We lived on Sand Mountain above Scottsboro, which has the same pristine views that you would find in the Smokey Mountains. There was no need for us to make a trip to Gatlinburg; we lived there. All we had to do was walk outside.

Dad rode the bike up to this opening and then shut it off. As he was getting off the motorcycle, my heart began to pound a bit, wondering what was about to take place. Had I done something wrong? Was someone sick and about to die? My mind was running away with me with thoughts, ideas, and concerns about what this impromptu meeting was about. I couldn't accept the notion that Dad just wanted to spend this moment with me.

I tried to relax and put on a face that nothing was wrong. It was tough.

On this particular Sunday afternoon, the weather was perfect— not too hot, not too cold. It was a picture-perfect day for a

motorcycle ride. At the age of thirteen, here I was sitting on top of a mountain overlooking a great view and just enjoying the fact that I was with my dad . . . just me and him. But I kept wondering what this was all about. I have never been singled out before.

We were not there long before I heard my dad's voice quiver as he began talking. I had no clue what was about to come out of his mouth. It was as though I quit breathing myself until he finished his statement. He continued to tell me, as best as he could, how he had promised my mom that when they thought I was old enough to understand, he would tell me something about my past that I have never considered or thought of before. It had to do with my biological dad.

My what? You mean the man I thought was my father for the past thirteen years is not my actual dad?

The words that proceeded out of his mouth were deafening. I, all of sudden, became numb. Even today, I remember word for word what he said to me as though it was recorded. All these years, it has been on a loop that has been forever playing in my mind.

He said, "I promised your mom that I would share this with you when we felt like you were old enough to understand. Your dad ran away when your mom found out she was pregnant with you. Now if you want to see him and meet him, I can take you to him right now. But, Mickey, I believe as God sees it, I am your dad and will forever be your dad."

Oh my gosh! How was I supposed to react to this kind of news? Was I supposed to be mad, or angry? Should I go and meet this

man who gave me life and then ran away from the responsibility? But in that moment, as a young teenage boy, I

was more concerned about the man who was just so honest with me that I didn't want to show any feelings whatsoever. That had to be hard on him to do.

For thirteen years, this man had to live with the fact in knowing this day would come. I can only imagine how many times it would cross his mind on how he would tell me. How many times he would rehearse what he would say. How he would imagine it would go, but more importantly, how I would react. Would this cause problems for our family? Would I wig out and become a handful?

I had heard later of other teens who lost their minds when they found out similar news. They started acting out in hopes of getting something. They started playing family members against each other.

Just as I remember the words that were shared with me on that day from my dad, I also remember what I said as a response.

"As far as I am concerned, you are my dad, and I never want to meet this other man."

After saying these words that I meant from the bottom of my

heart, I leaped over into my dad's arms, and he held me tighter than I had ever remembered before. And I was serious about what I said. I meant every word. I never wanted to talk about it again. And I didn't. I held true to this statement even until this day.

I am not sure if an announcement was made to everyone in the house, but we never spoke of it. I don't know if they talked

about it when I wasn't around. I am sure they did, but that was not my concern. I just knew the topic was not up for discussion as far as I was concerned.

But I can't sit here and say there weren't signs that made me wonder. I could look at the family pictures and tell that I was not like everyone else. I was the only dark-headed kid in the family. My brother and sisters had beautiful blond and brown hair. I was pushing five-foot-three while my brother was the star high school basketball player at six-seven. Quite a bit of difference.

I heard the jokes that I was pushed away from the table all my life. I was the butt of many jokes that I had to wear hand-me-downs from my younger brother. I was always the short one in the bunch. I get it. I just learned to live with that. It seems I got really good at living with heartache and pain but covering it up as though it never hurt me. In my mind, showing any emotion would give victory to the biological man who created me. So, I kept myself in a position to not let him win.

The real reason this unexpected news was so hard for me to believe was an actual tribute to my parents.

In the simple fact that my parents never treated me any differently when I was a child than any other sibling. There was never a time when I was referred to as being the son of someone else. It never came up when I was being punished, and

I AM DAVID!

Mickey Bell

I was never treated as an outsider to the family.

So, while I tried to be positive with the life-changing news I had just heard, now I had to process and try to understand what had happened. I meant what I said about meeting this man that I have never seen. I meant what I said about who my daddy was. I wish I could say that I never thought about it again, but it was something that would weigh heavy on me. Why the man who actually gave seed to bring me into this world didn't love me

enough to see me through this world? Why he felt the need to run instead of providing? Why he thought it was best to ignore me instead of pouring into me? What did I ever do to him?

How am I supposed to process this information at thirteen? Did my own father look at me as a mistake instead of a blessing? Was I going to cramp his style? Was my life going to hinder his? So, he just leaves me to fight through this world all by myself?

Would it be any different if I were sixteen or even twenty-six when I found out this life-changing news? All I knew was that I did not want to meet this man who gave up on me before I ever had the chance to make him proud of me. Since he didn't want me, I didn't want him. And what if he tries to locate me? What if I am out in public and this random stranger comes up and tries to tell me that he is my dad? I am not sure how I would react to that. So, fear and anxiety set in. And as always, I would not share these feelings with anyone. From a very young age, this man caused me to look over my shoulder everywhere I went. A problem that I have today.

For the next twenty-five years, I had the mind-set that if he didn't want me then, I didn't want him now. I was very stubborn when it came to this subject matter. I don't know if I was wrong for thinking this way, but this was just my response. People who knew my story could not understand why I didn't ever want to meet him. By having one conversation with him, I could get answers that could eventually save my life. Information like genetic issues, such as heart disease, diabetes, or cancer. Are there things in his life I should know about that could affect me? I just felt as though it was best not knowing. If it meant having to meet this guy and spend time with him, I was okay with just the surprises that come with not knowing. I am not sure what I was afraid of by meeting him. I felt in a sense that it would be a slap in the face of my parents if I tried to reach out, as though

they were not enough for me and that I needed him. Which was *not* the case!

It was weird in the sense that while I could talk about it on stage

in front of thousands, it was never talked about one-on-one. There have been many times I would be doing a youth event or even now a Sunday service and I will feel the inspiration from the Holy Spirit to share this portion of my life. But once I walked off stage, I didn't want to discuss it further. This was never a subject that was discussed in my presence. All you had to do was hint like you were going to dive into that subject, and I would shut you down quicker than you could spit.

I am so proud of the family God placed me in because they treated me just like there was never a story to tell. I was never posed as the outcast or the one who didn't belong. But that didn't change the way I felt when I was alone. To be so adamant about not talking about it, I wasn't as strong to fight off the feelings that were creeping in. How do you hate someone you don't even know?

I would later learn more about the man who gave me life, and I was glad that I did not have to battle the demons he had to fight in his own life. To this day, I cannot tell you his name or anything else about him, but this I do know, that man put more demons in me than he ever thought just by leaving me when he did. You heard me right, demons.

While I never got to know him or even had the chance to get attached to him, his departure out of my life gave birth to a demon of neglect that I never knew about. A force on the inside of me that would cause me to always want to please people in fear of anyone else walking out of my life. I would bend over backward and allow people to walk all over me. You could make fun of me, talk about me behind my back, or even stab me in the

back; just don't leave me, and I would be okay.

There are so many young people that I encounter daily who will have issues later in life if they don't take a hold of their thoughts

now. Different situations presented to them at a young age have caused them to encounter demons that are manipulating them to become someone they were never created to be.

I remember the day my wife, Wendy, came to me in tears. I was in my early thirties. She explained how she had something to tell me but didn't know how I would react. In that moment, she told me that my biological dad had died. Ummm, it was a weird feeling. I felt bad because of the fact that I didn't feel bad. Does that even make sense? I was bothered by the fact that I wasn't mourning his death. Then I got mad at him all over again because now I have unexplained feelings all because he couldn't stay and take the responsibility for what he had created . . . *me*!

I never saw a picture of him, so I don't know if I look like him. Since I was never around him, I don't know if I have traits that would remind others of him. Does my mom look at me and see

27

him? His decision to leave me afforded the enemy the opportunity to hold me captive with my thoughts to the point I didn't know how to deal with it. I was constantly looking for the affirmation of others, and it was never enough. To the point that my life was miserable, and it made my relationships even more difficult.

Oh, the power of affirmation that comes from the mouth of your father. Even though I had a man in my life who actually loved me enough to adopt me at birth when I wasn't his to begin with. Even though I had a mom who loved me with everything she had within her. Even though I had a wife who stuck with me through thick and thin. The need for affirmation

was never met because I never felt complete. I never felt like I was enough and the people in my life would always be looking for something better in which to leave me. And they normally left.

Wow! And then I become a pastor, which is the worst line of

work you could go into if you don't want to be let down by people. Ask my wife, and she would tell you that I never worried about paying the bills for the church. I was never stressed over budget meetings or the possibility of closing down the church.

I was always the person who could motivate anyone to do any-thing. But just give me a hint that you are about to leave or that I have let you down, and that would absolutely crush me. I had this need for everyone to like me, and if you didn't, I would lose sleep over it. My wife could never understand this about me, and I was never in a place where I felt like I could tell her. It was almost like opening a door that I never wanted to open. Not because of anything I had done but simply because of what the man did who gave me his seed.

I AM DAVID!

Mickey Bell

I guess what I am trying to tell you is this: "I am David. I know what it feels like to have your dad forget all about you and make you feel like you are not enough."

Don't tell me this is not a real struggle because these demons of affirmation are real, and they will torment your life and cause you to make decisions that are not in your best interest.

We have a generation of young men growing up without fathers. We have a group of girls growing up, that while their dad might have been present, they never felt his presence, and thus the roller-coaster ride of bad decisions in an attempt to fill that void. Now girls are running away with the first guy who tells them he loves them simply because they didn't have a dad in

their life to tell them. They allowed guys to treat them like trash due to the fact their dad was never there to demonstrate how a man was supposed to treat a woman. So, they assume that being hit is normal, just as long as you don't leave. Being cursed at and slammed up against the refrigerator is acceptable just as long as you stay with me. This is a wrong way of thinking for any

young woman, and if you are in this type of relationship, get help!

Now we have young girls who don't feel pretty enough, skinny enough, and they make unhealthy decisions that could be fatal.

We have forty-year old boys who are now supposed to be men, but they never had anyone to show them what being a man was all about. They can't keep a relationship because they don't know how to provide. They don't have the respect of the kids since he has not been there to be a dad. Who is going to teach them if their own dad wasn't present? How many would not be in prison today if dad would have just stayed home? How many would not be addicted to vices in their life if their dad would have just showed his love instead of presupposing that is was felt?

We have young men growing up without the affirmation of their fathers marrying young women who do not understand the love of a man because she didn't have her father, and we expect that marriage to work? Neither was able to witness how the man is supposed to love the wife. So, they are going into this relationship blind, and we are shocked that more than 50 percent of marriages are ending in divorce.

Many know what it's like to not be included every time you played pickup games on the playground. Remember when you had team captains who would begin choosing teams and you

had to stand there long enough for it to come down between you and the only girl playing that day.

David had to deal with not making the first round of picks by his dad. I had to deal with not being enough for my seed donor to even stick around. What's your struggle? I'm not asking what your symptoms are, but the cause of the pain you are dealing with. You know what you do, but do you know why you are

doing it? You know you are hurting, and you know the decisions you have been making, but what causes you to act and react the way you do?

While hearing our stories, what stronghold has been brought to light that you have kept hidden in the darkest areas of your heart and mind? I know you said you would never deal with it again. In fact, you have kept it hidden for so long that it doesn't hurt as much anymore. You have bought into the lie from Satan that real men don't share their feelings.

I AM DAVID!

Mickey Bell

When Christ came back for the death of his friend Lazarus, he asked the question, "Where have you laid him?" And when Jesus walked up to the tomb, he said, "Move the stone." Move what you have put into place, so you don't have to constantly look at what hut you. And for many, you have moved away from the moment that is the source of your pain that it doesn't hurt as much as it used to hurt you.

You have moved to a different relationship and think you are free and clear when you never dealt with the real problem. You keep jumping from one marriage to the next. One job to another. You keep moving from one church to another church every time the pressure is on you to deal with these emotions.

You just keep hiding it as though if you don't look at it, then it won't affect you. But it still does. Just because the stone is

there doesn't mean that death didn't take place. But can we admit to each other that even though you have kept it covered up for a long time, there are still moments when the pain or the hurt starts to come back in?

When you fly off the handle at the smallest things, when you yell at your kids when they didn't do anything wrong, when you cry, and you don't even know why you are crying. You can either

do some- thing about it or continue to live with these distractions in your life. But there's a problem that I must tell you about that will save your life if you will listen to me. Based on the church where you were raised, this information may scare you a bit. It was not something that I learned in my church growing up, so it took time for me to fully understand. It's the process in which you received the heartache had a demon attached to it.

31

The Bible says, "We wrestle not against flesh and blood but against the principalities of the air." Since you are not familiar with this subject matter, you think demon possession is only concentrated to people who flop on the floor uncontrollably while foaming at the mouth. This is only something you would hear about happening at the Pentecostal church on Thursday nights.

There is also this belief that you can't be controlled by a demon if you belong to Christ. Let me put it this way: while you can't be possessed by a demon, you are definitely influenced.

Throughout God's Word, we are confronted with people who are dealing with spirits that have overtaken them. And such is the case with people today. We have just played into the enemy's hand when we want to overlook this as a serious, viable reason we do what we do. So, if you are making bad decisions, what or

who is making you do that?

The Word teaches us how these things can be considered generational curses. That's why a doctor's visit will have you answering questions about your ancestors. Did your grandparents have heart disease? Are your parents diabetics? Things are handed down from generation to generation.

And if you look closely, you will see how this trait that is causing you such pain in your life has been handed down from

generation to generation. It might not have started with you, and it certainly didn't stop with you. Until you remove this stronghold from your life, you are promising your little girl and your little boy that you will be passing this on to them.

And if you are a parent or soon to be one, please know your next generation is operating with the power you give them. This could be something positive or something painful and negative. And the demons you don't deal with as an adult right now will one day be passed on to your children and your grandchildren. But not only for the sake of your children, you should deal with this so the remainder of your days can be joyous.

For some reading my story, you may have had a dad who was present, but you never felt his presence. He might have been there in body, but he was never there in spirit. He might have been there to see you off to bed or carry you to your sports game or practice, but you are dealing with a spirit that is demanding more affirmation simply because you didn't get it at home.

Many more kids are growing up in single-parent homes.

While your dad didn't express his love for you, now you are looking for any man to tell you how beautiful you are even if it is

the wrong man. Now you might be twice divorced, wondering what is wrong with you. It's not really you; it's the spirit of abandonment that you have within you. And until you deal with this demon, you will continue to look for love in all the wrong places. You will continue to allow people to abuse you while you sit and take it because you don't know what affirmation looks or feels like.

If you ignore the information, I will be sharing with you, not only will you grow up without affirmation, but you will also raise up another generation that doesn't know how important their voice really is.

But keep reading because there is a way to be set free!

CHAPTER 3
When You're Not Invited to the Party

David is having to deal with the fact that while he works just as hard as his brothers, he was not chosen to be in the lineup. His dad didn't see him as important enough to make the cut. So, he had to deal with his emotions on the spot.

Standing out in a field with nothing but stinky sheep, David is running through his mind what he did wrong. Was he not tall enough? Was he not good enough?

Why wouldn't his dad include him in the lineup of the boys he was proud of? OMG, Is Jesse not proud of David?

What this shepherd boy didn't realize was that this would be one of many times he would have to be separated from others because of the purpose of his life. God's plan for him might not have been recognized by others, but it would bring good days and bad days in his life. This is the first lesson David encounters when learning to live out the text, "Come out from among them and be ye separate."

So, what do you do when you are different on purpose and the calling on your life pushes you away from people instead of surrounding you with friends who get it? Every person created by God is done so with a purpose.

That is why the abortion issue is close to my heart. My mom had a choice when the man she loved was about to leave her because of me. She could have made the decision that she loved him more than me; therefore, I could have become a statistic. I could have become a baby with a purpose that was aborted before I had the time to fulfill my destiny.

Whether it was a thought that she had or a decision that was never challenged with her emotions, my mom chose me over him. She allowed him to leave so she could bring me into this world.

But that is not always the case. If we truly believe that every child is created with a purpose, then how many answers to our prayers were killed the moment we aborted a child? The last baby that was just aborted, did he have the cure to cancer? The baby that was aborted last week, was she the one who could have stopped Down syndrome? We will never know because when we took the life, we also forfeited the purpose.

David is stuck out in the field all alone, having to deal with his thoughts and emotions of not being invited to the party that was taking place in his own home.

A young boy with a great purpose, but no friends. A shepherd with a promising future but left out in the cold.

How do you handle having such a powerful purpose that it causes you to be rejected by others instead of them praising the rea- son you are here? I AM DAVID!

Looking back on my childhood, there were things that matched up to the lives of those being raised around me, but then there were things that made me different. I am not talking about the height difference between me and my brother. I am not talking about being the only kid in the family with dark hair. I liken it unto the scripture in Jeremiah 1:5 when the Lord says, "Before I formed you, I knew you."

I can relate to that text in the fact that I had callings from God on my life from an early age. That made growing up in my skin a bit tougher than the other kids my age simply because my values and goals were different, even before my teen years.

People all around us knew that we were church going people. The coaches for my youth sporting leagues knew that if they scheduled a practice or a game on church night, I would be at church. That's just the way it was.

It all started the night I accepted Christ as my Savior. My family was returning home from a Sunday night singing at our church. Those were always my favorite, and you will find why in just a moment. Mom and Dad would pile five kids and Granny Bell into the car for our thirty-minute trip one way to our home church.

So, to entertain us kids, we would have sing-alongs to make the trip seem shorter. There were no CD players, or satellite radios that allowed you to be picky about the music that you played in the car. This meant that we had to provide our own Christian family entertainment.

Such was the case on this particular Sunday night when the Holy Spirit started dealing with me about my salvation. At eight years old, I didn't have this burning testimony of being delivered from drugs or alcohol. In fact, I didn't know of any issues that I had because as you may recall, I am not thirteen yet, so the news I shared with you in the last chapter hasn't happened yet.

The Bell choir was singing on the way home from church when the words to this song pierced my heart: "Sorry I never knew you." The song dealt with a man who had died and gone to heaven only to find out that his name was not written down in the Book of Life as confirmation of accepting Christ while here

Mickey Bell

on earth.

> Last night as I lay sleeping a dream came to
> me, I dreamed about the end of time, about
> eternity. I saw a million sinners fall on their
> knees to pray. The Lord he sadly shook His
> head, and this I heard Him say.

> Chorus

> Sorry I never knew you; I find no record of
> your birth.

> Sorry I never knew you; go and serve the one
> that you have served before.

The song goes on to tell the story of how this guy was asking God to please check the book again. He was sure he had taken the time to accept Christ and his name was recorded.

It was in that moment, I started feeling the tug at my heart concerning my salvation. Even though I was only eight years old, I knew the difference between right and wrong. My family had me and my siblings in church every time the church doors were open. My church believed in two services on Sunday—one service on Wednesday and support all the other churches during their revival meetings during the week. Back then, the churches didn't plan their meetings around the ball schedule like many do today.

Oh no, the revival meetings were planned, and church was placed in the forefront over all other activities. And when it came to revival meetings, we didn't have these one-night services or a weekend revival meeting. These services were

Monday through Friday with the option to extend to another week if necessary.

So, being the young age of eight was no problem for the Holy

Spirit because I had enough of the Word already inside of me for him to work with.

I remember as though it happened yesterday. We were headed up Sand Mountain on Highway 40 to take Granny Bell home. I recall leaning up from the back seat to tell my mom that I needed to be *saved*, which is a term used in a lot of churches to describe a person who has never repented of their sins and committed their life to Jesus Christ.

Since she was in the front seat, I was unable to see her face, but I can only imagine what that must feel like to have your child come to that realization. She simply said these words: "Let's wait until we get home."

Wait until we get home? As a young kid, I was afraid in that moment that we would never make it home. And if I died before we got to the house, I would be burning in a lake of fire, which I heard so much about.

Well, God answered my prayer—no, not for salvation but that we made it home safe and sound. Once we entered into the front door, I immediately ran to my dad and told him that I needed him to pray with me. We knelt down at one of those ugly brown 1980s couches that seemed to be in style at the time. There, as an eight-year- old boy, I poured my heart out to God like I had thirty years of sin that needed to be removed from my life.

I can still remember the feeling I felt when God touched me. I can still close my eyes and take myself back to that precious moment that I had with my family the night I made Jesus Christ my Savior. What a moment. To be surrounded by all my brother and sisters. To have parents who took the time to pray with me.

I can remember exactly what I told my dad when he asked me how I felt. I said these words: "I feel like the dark clouds have been replaced with blue skies."

I know that may not be very deep, but give me a break, I was only eight years old . . . geez. I couldn't wait to tell everybody. The joy of the Lord that filled my little heart wanted to tell the world. So, I started with my grandparents and then my pastor.

No one had to tell me what the next step for me would be. It was time to get baptized. I couldn't wait to get to church the next Sunday so I could walk forward to let the world know what God did for me in my living room.

After walking down, the aisle of my church, I was escorted a few weeks later into the Tennessee River, where I was baptized. No baptisteries during this time—no, we gathered by the river just as the song said.

It was in that moment that a path for my life would be created. A path that would have me experiencing things that other kids my age would not experience. A path that would have me looking at life differently than others my age. Not because I am now a Christian, but because I had passed the first test of trusting God with my future.

The moment he spoke with instruction, I was willing to listen and obey. Little did I know that this was the first of many encounters I would have with God concerning my life and relationship with Him.

I AM DAVID!

What I haven't told you about life up until this point was my love for gospel music. Not just any gospel music, but southern gospel music. For some reason, I was attracted to the quartet and trio sounds of groups with live bands. In fact, I loved it so much that

I committed that as my life's dream. I longed for the day when I could crawl onto a quartet bus and travel the world, being on stage and playing gospel music.

At this young age, I wasn't thinking about any other type of music. Oh no, it had to be southern gospel music. I can remember lying in my bed one Christmas Eve praying to God for a stereo. I even made a deal with him. I told God that if he would give me a stereo system, I would play nothing but southern gospel music on it. I think I kept my word because that was the only type of music I wanted to hear.

I know now that it's not the most popular genre of music to enjoy. It is many times looked down on as a dying breed of music, but it was my music that appealed to me. I not only loved it then, but it still speaks to me now.

I was so committed to this genre of music. Instead of *Sports Illustrated*, I would stand at the mailbox, waiting for the gospel music trade magazines to arrive. Then for the next month, I would put to memory everything that was contained inside.

In my preteen years, I could tell you every gospel group that was promoted on those pages. I knew where they lived, the color of the bus they drove, and for the most part, I could name every person in the group and tell you distinctive things about each one. I would memorize the chart and could tell you the top ten songs without taking a breath. I could hear the introduction to a song on the radio and tell you the song and artist before they even began singing.

I AM DAVID!

Mickey Bell

I was eaten up with it!

So many groups I could name from that era. The Hinsons, the Paynes, and the Cathedrals.

There was a group known as the Kingsmen Quartet. They were very exciting to watch on stage, but they were known for their live recordings. My parents knew that if you wanted to make me happy, just buy me the latest Kingsmen cassette, and I would be one happy boy.

For those of you that don't know, cassette tapes were these rectangular pieces of plastic that would . . . never mind. It was just the way we listened to music back then.

I would get these "live" recordings and listen to them so much that I had them memorized. Not just the songs, but every word that was said on that tape. I could introduce the members of the group just as good as Big Jim Hamill did.

With such a large family, our vacations were really short-day trips or maybe an overnight stay in a camping resort. I can remember going to what was known as Opryland in Nashville, Tennessee.

This theme park that surrounded the legends of country music would turn their stages over to the southern gospel artists. So, every Labor Day weekend, my family would take me to see my favorites. While my brother and sisters were riding the rides, I was sitting in front of the stage, starstruck as each artist came up to sing.

I had a cousin named Ronnie who was quite older than I was. He was able to drive, so he would always carry me to the Boutwell Auditorium in Birmingham, Alabama, to the all-night gospel singings. Back then, you could take in your cassette players and record the concerts. I don't know if it was legal or not, so we didn't ask. Ronnie made sure I got a copy of every artist.

There is no way to tell you how many hours I would sit in my room and play this music, and just dream that it was me on that

stage. I can remember coming home from concerts and crying myself to sleep while praying to God that He would allow me to travel and do what I saw others doing.

Instead of having pictures on my wall of Alabama football players or the hottest rock band, I had pictures of the Kingsmen (my favorite), the Nelons, Gold City, and the Commandments. The Commandments were a family group from Hartselle that I had on my wall because I had a crush on the girl that played bass and sang. It didn't matter that she was ten years older than me and her boyfriend played the drums is she made the wall!

My memories also recall Sunday mornings in the Bell house. We would always wake up to a breakfast that included homemade biscuits and chocolate gravy. If you have not experienced chocolate gravy, then you don't know what you are missing. Just make sure you are saved because I have asked God to make sure that chocolate gravy be served at the marriage supper of the Lamb.

Every Sunday after breakfast, I would hurry to my room to get dressed for church. I had to hurry because I had a date with the television before we headed out for 10:00 AM service.

Dad would always make sure the television was on the same station every week. That is when Jimmy Swaggart would come on. He had the best music to start your day. Watching those musicians and listening to John Starnes and Janet Pascal was the highlight of my morning—well, besides the chocolate gravy.

I AM DAVID! Mickey Bell

After the music portion was complete, I would never stick around to listen to the preaching. I would hurry off to the car ahead of the family so I could turn on the radio. No matter what type of music was played during the week, the stations in Alabama would play gospel music on Sundays.

This was back before praise and worship or any contemporary competition. So, if gospel music was on the air, there was only one style they played—southern gospel music, and that was fine with me.

Jerry Gentle was the man in Scottsboro who would feed into my love for this music. I would always call him to request the song that I needed to record. And just as soon as I heard, "This next song is going out too little Mickey," I would hit Play/Record to capture the moment. Later on, in my teen years, Tim Maze would keep me up to date on the latest hits with his Sunday morning gospel radio show.

It was no secret to anyone that I loved this music.

While noticing my love for music, my parents invested into my future. They did something not many others would do for the sake of their sanity. They saw my attraction to the drums and purchased me a snare drum. No, not a full set because I was only eight years old. I never took a lesson, and when you listened to me play, you didn't have to be convinced otherwise.

I actually graduated up to the snare drum from my homemade set. I was notorious for going to the kitchen and pulling out the pots and pans to create my own version of a drum set. Even in church, I would set up my hymnals to mimic what I saw on stage. And there every Sunday morning, Sunday night, and Wednesday night, I put on my own concert.

The day came when my parents allowed me to take my snare drum to church to become a part of the church band. I need to go ahead and apologize to all those who attended Pathway Baptist Church during this time of my life. Those people had to be very special to allow a kid to hit a snare drum during their worship services.

What great memories I was able to create. I had my snare drum set up in church right behind the piano that my mom played every service. I didn't know what I was doing, and I probably got on the nerves of those in the church, but in my mind, I was on one of the biggest stages every weekend, dreaming of one day doing this for real.

I don't remember my exact age, but I want to say I was about ten years old when my dad came home from work one Saturday with a huge surprise. When he pulled into our driveway, Mom asked me to go and help him unload his work truck. I would like to tell you that as a saved ten-year-old boy, I jumped at the opportunity to honor my father and mother with a pure heart. Needless to say, I might have been a saved future gospel musician, but I was still a ten-year-old brat.

Reluctantly, I made my way outside to only find that my parents had purchased me a full set of drums. I know you are reading this and you find this to be so minute that you can't believe I am making a big deal about it in this book, but you have to understand, this was the next step of my dream coming true.

This was like David getting his slingshot for Christmas. This was like Michael Jordan getting a basketball. This was like President Trump getting his red MAGA hat. This was *huge* (said in my Trump voice).

That small sparkly blue set of drums was the best thing in my life. I could not get them in the house quick enough. Since I had been watching groups with drummers all my life, no one had to show me how to set them up. I didn't need a book or anyone else for that matter to tell me how they should be placed.

Within moments, I had my cassette player hooked up, and I was playing on stage with the Kingsmen. There I was, sitting next to

the ugly brown couch that served as my altar. I had Anthony Burger on one side playing the piano, Gary "Beaver" Dillard on the steel guitar, and Big Jim Hamill taking us through many concerts that my family would hear on the stage we called our living room.

It wasn't long before the drums were removed from our home and taken to our local church. Once I showed my parents that I was able to keep a steady beat, I was able to set up on our church stage, where I would play every Sunday morning, Sunday night, and Wednesday night . . . and every revival meeting. I played *a lot*!

Our church was a southern-gospel-music-loving church. Every fourth Sunday night, a different quartet or trio would make their way to our church for an evening concert, and for me, that was better than attending an Alabama football game. We went to a very lively church, so adding a full service was always a treat.

It was a bonus for me if they ever arrived without having a drummer in the group. Many times, they would hear me playing for the congregational music to kick off the service and would ask me to sit in with them. OMG! I miss those days.

At the age of ten, a trio came to our church, and what do you know? They wanted me to sit in with them. But something happened after the service that I never dreamed would happen. They asked my parents if it would be okay if I traveled with them every- where they went.

Are you kidding me? I get to travel and play music? I don't have to just lie on my bed at night and beg God in my prayers, but I can actually go and play? I had no idea this was coming. I just had in my mind that I would be out of high school before an opportunity like this would present itself.

God had heard my prayer. He knew the desires of my heart.

They didn't have a bus, but it didn't matter. Every time I crawled into the van; in my mind I was stepping on to a silver eagle bus. My life was consumed with traveling and playing music. My first group, the Heritage Trio, was very popular in the area churches. It was nothing for us to sing two and three times every weekend. At ten years old, I was away from my family a lot while playing. I never got scared, and I never gave it a second thought. It was just something I was born to do.

I never got tired, and I never missed a singing.

Those were some of the best moments in my life. From age ten to nineteen, my life was consumed with playing music. Now don't get me wrong, I took part in a few things in school, such as the marching band and junior high sports. But the stage of a gospel music concert was where I was meant to be.

I was so dedicated to this part of my life that I even skipped my junior and senior prom simply because I had a concert on those dates. Oh, my date was so mad at me. Nothing, not even girls, was getting in the way of me being on stage and playing music.

Looking back on that time in my life, I can see now that I was left out of a lot of things. I wasn't invited to the parties at school. I was not in the "in" crowd.

Other teens were not impressed with my dream of being a southern gospel musician. They didn't understand, nor did they get it, but they didn't have too.

It was my dream, and that was all I thought about. Just like David, I know what it is like to be set aside because you are different. I am not saying that I was more important, not at all. I

was just different. God had a purpose for my life, but because of dreams and aspirations, high school was not the best time for me.

I had moments of good times, but not even my family knows until now what a struggle it was for me. I wasn't tempted with drugs, and I never attempted to try alcohol. The struggle was simply in the fact that I didn't fit in. Put me on a stage in front of thousands, and I am happy. Sit me in a desk in high school or make me walk down the hallways, and I was terrified. I was picked on and made fun of. I was bullied before "bullies" were known and dealt with.

To say that I didn't notice how the pretty girls always hung out with the athletes would be lie. I was connected to my music, but I still liked girls and I always felt like I had to have one in my life, but I wasn't anyone's pick by any stretch of the imagination and being gone every weekend didn't help the dating status either.

This all took place before I was thirteen, which means I was already feeling secluded before the Sunday afternoon meeting with my dad. I was already feeling the pressure of making choices that was not popular with those I was around.

My dreams had me going to places that other kids my age were not even wanting to go to. Other kids were kicking and screaming not wanting to go to church. I was going four or five times a week and loving it, as long as I was playing music.

Other kids could not understand why I loved it so much, and I couldn't put it into words to help them understand. So, there I was . . . different on purpose. I was getting what I really wanted, but it was coming with a price.

I started learning at a very young age that ministry was a very

lonely place.

Pastors reading this portion of the book know exactly what I'm talking about. The congregation loves you at the church building but don't really want to associate with you outside of the services. They feel the need to clean up their act when you are around, so they just choose to leave you out and alone. It's just too much trouble for many of them to live right while you are around, so they just as soon leave you home alone.

While others are gathering for a day at the river, the pastor and his family are many times left alone at home. Families within the church have grown up together and have a special bond. The pastor is just someone who has been brought in, and no matter how long you are there, you will always be an outsider to them. When the elder tells you that he will be there longer than you, he is prophesying, and he is right!

I can't tell you how many nights my family of three has stayed at home to only find out on social media that there was a gathering that we were not told about. I am just saying that ministry can be a very lonely place, and no one really understands that until you have been a pastor.

So, what do you do when you are different on purpose and the calling on your life pushes you away from people instead of surrounding you with friends who get it?

Our friend David knows exactly how we feel. It's not friends that are pushing him out, but his own family has overlooked him. He is so talented with his music. He is so committed to being a good shepherd, but that gets him nowhere when it comes to being invited inside his own house by his own father.

CHAPTER 4
Looks Aren't Everything

> But the Lord said unto Samuel, look not on his countenance, or on the height of his stature; because I have refused him: for the Lord seeth not as man seeth; for man looketh on the out- ward appearance, but the Lord looketh on the heart.
>
> —1 Samuel 16:7

The prophet Samuel did as the Lord asked him to do. He went and took a look at the young men put in front of him by Jesse. While this father thought his older more mature boys were surely the pick for the next king, he was taught a very valuable lesson that you need to learn as well.

God does not approve you based on your outward appearance. And if we fully captured this concept, what would we be like if we worked on us inside like we work to fix up our outside?

What if we would spend time each morning decorating our inside with the time we take to shave, apply makeup, shower, and fix our hair? We say we don't have time to start our morning with the Word, yet we have plenty of time to start it with Maybelline.

The enemy is very crafty when it comes to luring you into the game of comparison. And it starts at a very young age when young children who are not yet able to speak complete sentences. Just put one in the floor with the toy of their choice and then later add another child with a different toy. The first child will want what is not his based on the fact that it's something new. The attraction of something that is newer, shinier, or more appealing.

That same trick is used on us mentally and emotionally. The devil attempts to take our own looks and use it against us by constantly putting others beside us in the form of comparison. We are not as tall. We are not as pretty. We are not as athletic. We are not as talented.

Comparison to others will have you slumping down into depression if you are not careful. It will cause you to discount yourself and the positive attributes you contain. You might be considered God's creation, but you hate what you see. Not because of your own thought but based on how others are comparing you to what they think is normal or successful.

Why do you think teen girls starve themselves to look like the models that have been photoshopped? Why are guys in the gym trying to get buff? Who told you that you needed to lose 20 pounds when you weigh 110?

I am not sure if David had to deal with this emotionally or mentally before this event, but he sure had to face it when Samuel the prophet came to town. It seems that this event, on this day, has everything to do with outer appearance. He sees his father beaming with pride as he presents his older brothers, and he sees himself left outside, not measuring up.

What if this wasn't the only time David had to deal with rejection from his father? Could it be that we don't have it recorded how many times Jesse chose his older brothers over David? You may say, "Wait a minute, you are trying to add to the Word." Well, the text never told us that they ate a meal or took a bath, but we hope they did both.

I know how boys can be when they are away from their parents.

Don't think for one second that David never got teased for being the youngest. Don't even try to bypass the fact that he was picked on and made fun of because he was the baby of the family.

Don't forget about his set of chores. The shepherd was the lowest of the lows. Boys can be mean, and don't kid yourself into think- ing that David never had to deal with the enemy of comparison.

What do you think David was thinking while out in the field? He is having to continue to work while his brothers are being paraded in front of everyone else. They get a break while he has to continue to work.

"It's not fair that I am having to still do my chores and my brothers are in the house doing God-knows-what!"

"What is so wrong with me that they don't feel like I am good enough to be brought in?"

"What did I do to deserve being shunned by my own dad and family?"

I know how he feels because . . . I AM DAVID.

This is going to be tough for me to share since this is the first time I have ever dealt with these thoughts and feelings, but I can attest to the feelings of David.

Being the adopted son in the family, I was always compared to a bloodline that I was never a part of. My features as a young boy were constantly recognized while I was with my family.

I AM DAVID!   Mickey Bell

My brother Paul, whom I love dearly, was a beast in high school.

Having the seed of the Bell family, he was tall and massively built. In many cases, throughout his sports career, he was a man among boys. I can remember many times during T-ball games, my parents would have to present a birth certificate just to prove that he was only eight years old. It always seemed to happen after he got up to bat and hit the ball into the next county!

As Paul continued to mature through high school, his ability in sports only increased with his size and mind. Not only was he athletic, but Paul was very smart. That has carried him far in life.

He was six-seven in high school and became the very first athlete at Section High School to receive a four-year athletic scholarship to a university, and things didn't stop there for him. He went on to start as a freshman in college and ended up breaking the school's all- time scoring record at Lee University in Cleveland, Tennessee. They have already retired his jersey number, and he's not even dead yet. They don't do that for guys who are only five feet six inches tall.

I love my brother. And I probably haven't told him enough how proud I am of him but growing up under him with me being the older brother was tough. Our sizes were always being compared with me being the "runt" of the jokes. Even when we played backyard ball with *my* friends who are my age, they were always picking him first. I don't blame them one bit. He was a very good athlete, and his team always won. Heck, I always wanted to be on his team.

When it came to family picture time, I hated the thought of dealing with the next photographer who thought he was going to be cute and funny. Because as you know, the tallest and what would normally be the oldest would go in the back. Not in our case. I was always put in the front, which messed with my mind.

The jokes were always the same: "Did Paul push you away from the table?" "I bet you have to wear his hand-me-downs." "What happened to you, Mickey?"

I would just attempt to laugh it off until I got alone and then deal with the pain of the comparison, and then getting older didn't help when it came to high school filled with teenagers who can be so cruel at times. It only took one to wise up to what was happening and speak without even knowing: "Hey, Mickey, are you adopted or something?" It was tough being the runt of the family.

At a moment when all the others were shooting up in height, I was staying the same. High school was not a great place for a boy who wanted to play music in the gospel field. It was all about the sports, and who could take us to the playoffs. Don't get me wrong, it wasn't the fault of my classmates or even the adults who were all a part of our lives. They just didn't know about my abandonment issues due to my biological dad, and then to be rejected constantly because of comparisons made life worse.

Now maybe you can understand why I am always careful when I approach people. Just because they laugh while you are present doesn't always mean they are laughing when you leave.

As I look back on my life now, I feel that is why I threw myself into my music. When I went on stage, it didn't matter how tall I wasn't or what issues I had to deal with privately. I was in the spot- light, and the applause was partly for me and the effort I was giving to put on a good show. I was the cute little kid who played music, and it drew a lot of attention. A lot of attention that I wasn't getting anywhere else.

I AM DAVID!

I guess that is why I never thought of doing anything else. I could get on a bus and travel away from my hometown to see people

who didn't know me, or would care what I am not. They didn't know that my younger brother was a full foot taller than me. They didn't know that I was the only black-haired kid in the family. They didn't know my dad left me before I was ever born. They would just accept me for who I am, and come on, I was adorable sitting on stage as the young one.

Comparisons are tough to deal with. On one side, people can understand what you are going through, and then on the other side, people will try to say you are just being jealous, but I have to disagree. Jealousy is me wanting to have what someone else has. That wasn't the case for me. It wasn't that I desired the height of my brother. It wasn't that I wished for the athletic abilities of others. I just simply wanted to be accepted for who I was. Is that so much to ask?

I just wanted to be okay in my own skin, but the comparison of others made that very difficult. Remarks from people who were trying to be funny were adding layers of pain.

It was just the simple fact that I couldn't be okay with me since no one else accepted me for me. I always thought I had to overcompensate to get people to accept me. Keep in mind, my dad had left me before I had the chance to prove myself, so what made me think others wouldn't do the same?

We don't think the kid who is overweight doesn't know he is bigger than everyone else?

We don't think the person with the different skin color feels different than his surroundings.

Yet instead of being accepting with open arms, we compare them to what we think they should be. But who gave us the authority to determine what is normal?

That's why we have so much debt in our country. People are not content with what they have, and they feel the need to keep up with everyone else. That's why we are paying for houses we really can't afford. We are driving cars that cost more than most people's houses. That's why you have to have designer jeans and make sure you take selfies eating at finer restaurants.

You have to stand in line to get the latest cell phone the moment it's available. We have parents who will half kill themselves just so their kids can look the part of something they are not.

The enemy knows that comparison will cause you to worry more about what others think about you, rather than what you and God thinks about you. That is when we start taking it a step further by allowing the comparisons to cause us to become fake people.

We are faking our happiness to be accepted. So, we fake our way around people, making them think we are okay when we are really dying on the inside. We can't admit we need help because we are being compared to people who we think are perfect.

The enemy causes us to buy into the lie that no one else is dealing with these issues that have us so consumed. To admit that I have issues will cause even more comparison to come upon me, and I just can't handle that.

Pastors know what I am talking about as well. You can't make people come to your church, but you are compared to the other churches who have more in attendance. Why do you think the numbers are always inflated? Why do you think we strive to look like we have more than we really have?

Church committees don't help you reach others for Christ, but they compare your success to how many people are attending.

Why do you think more pastors are quitting every day? It's because we can't win.

We are in constant comparison, and if we are not being compared to the church down the street, we are being compared to the favorite pastor who is no longer at the church. There will always be one who visited more or preached a lot better.

Don't get me started yet on being compared to your decisions and mistakes you make. Oh my, that is another therapy session wait- ing to happen!

Comparisons come in all shapes and sizes, but the most dangerous one of them all is when you stand in the mirror to compare your- self. No pain from others will compare to the pain you can inflict on yourself.

Looking into a reflection that you start disliking simply because others are not as accepting. Glaring intently into the eyes of a person who has been put down simply because of how God created you. That's tough to digest sometimes.

Who do you talk to about these issues? Who can you go to as a teen in the late eighties and share your feelings? In today's society, we are all about sharing our feelings with each other, but back then, you simply had to suck it up and just deal with it.

Or you can do what I did and just keep it bottled up on the inside, which allows it to just sit there and take root. Trust me, by the time you read the outcome at the end of this book, you will see why keeping it to yourself is not such a great idea. I wish I could say that "I am David" in the sense that I had a

heart for God. I thought I did, and it was easy to convince myself that I did since I was dealing with a genre of music that carried

the powerful message known as the gospel.

I was simply a young teenage boy who was looking for relief. I was trying to find myself in a world surrounded by others whom I had convinced myself didn't know what I was dealing with. I wanted someone to come and poke me with a needle just so the pain and discomfort would just leak out of me.

I wanted the feeling I had as a teenager to be gone; I just didn't know how to make it disappear. The only time the pain would dis- appear for me was when I was on stage in front of people with the spotlight shining down on me. It was in those moments when I felt like I was being accepted for who I was, and for not what I wasn't.

I wonder if David had these types of feelings? I wonder if he ever got lonely out in the sheep field where he caught himself talking to animals that were the only ones around who would listen?

Do you think David ever got to the point that he felt so neglected that you could hear him screaming out his frustrations, or do you think he just kept it all inside until a day later in his life when he has to deal with the pain all over again?

I can answer that question for you because . . . I am David.

Let me take this quick moment to encourage someone who is reading this book right now who is bound by comparisons. On the outside, David might have been smaller than his brothers, but on the inside, he was a born leader. On the outside, he didn't measure up to the other contestants; but on the inside, he was already chosen.

On the outside, he was nasty from doing what he was supposed to be doing; but on the inside, he was a king!

I don't need you to judge yourself based on what you see on the outside. It's the purpose you have on the inside that is separating you from the crowd.

On the outside you may look like a woman who has been beat down by another man but what you don't see on the inside is another man called the Holy Spirit who is raising you back up.

You may look into the mirror and see an alcoholic, or drug user that people have been talking about for years. You have been the butt of many jokes. You have been the topic of discussions on how people can't believe you would do that to your family, but on the inside, you are clean and overcoming what has been overtaking you.

On the outside, it may appear that you are deep in debt with no hope of seeing a brighter tomorrow, but on the inside, God is working with you to come out on the other side. On the outside, you may look depressed and lonely; but on the inside, you are more than a conqueror. On the outside you may look like you are defeated; but on the inside, you are a winner! On the outside, you may look like what I have been through; but on the inside, you look like where you are going!

Can someone just praise God for a moment for the fact that while people want to compare you based on how you look on the outside, God knows your heart and His purpose for you is far greater than what people could ever imagine? Can someone just thank God for the fact that while others gave up on you based on what they saw, God kept fighting for you based on what He has planted inside of you?

I know how David feels in this moment of his life, but I can also hear him saying, "If you look at my outward appearance you may have never chosen me to serve because I look and smell

like sheep, but what you don't realize is that on the inside, I am a king!"

"For the Lord seeth not as man seeth; for man looketh on the outward appearance, but the Lord looketh on the heart" (1 Samuel 16:7).

CHAPTER 5
Anointed, But Not Appointed

> So, he sent for him and had him brought in. He was glowing with health and had a fine appearance and handsome features. Then the Lord said, "Rise and anoint him; this is the one." So, Samuel took the horn of oil and anointed him in the presence of his brothers, and from that day on the Spirit of the Lord came power- fully upon David. Samuel then went to Ramah.
>
> —1 Samuel 16:12–13

The prophet Samuel took the time to evaluate each son of Jesse. He stood them up, front and center, while looking them up and down. Each time, each son, the man of God never felt the touch of the Holy Spirit that any of these guys were the one. And Jesse couldn't understand why none of his sons were being considered.

When looking on the outside, his boys were the poster child when it comes to being a prospect for the next king of Israel, but as we learned in the last chapter, a king is not appointed based on out- ward appearance. It's based on what you possess on the inside.

Looking cute won't win your battles when you are in war!

So, the prophet Samuel questions Jesse to see if there were any other boys. Thank God he asked for a recount!

Samuel was close enough to God with his relationship to be put on a task of this importance. For him, to be so sure that he was in the right town at the right house, he was not leaving until his job was done. Even if that meant he had to ask again for all the sons to be brought forth.

While the brothers knew that David was still out in the field and while Jesse had forgotten about his own son who was out doing his chores, the man of God perceived that the king had not been brought before him. So, he asked again.

Notice 1 Samuel 16:11 what the dad says about his son. For many of you, this would be a moment where you read right over these words and not think anything about it. But for those of us who have dealt with the pain of comparison and abandonment, these words leap off the pages.

Samuel asked, "Are these all your sons."

Jesse responds, "Well, there is one more, but he is the youngest, and he is too busy tending the sheep."

Ouch! David's father confirms there being another son, but Jesse doesn't think he is old enough to be considered. I have another son, but he is just a baby. I have another son, but he is not tall enough. I have another son, but he wouldn't measure up when you compare him to my other boys.

I have another son, but all he does is tend sheep. He is not important enough. He is not capable enough to be considered. Here, take a look at my other boys who can do so much more. They would be more beneficial to you than David. He is just a babysitter for our sheep.

Jesse made the same mistake that many fathers make today. They presuppose the purpose for their children. That's why many girls are pushed into beauty pageants to be crowned as queens, but they would never seek the affirmation of others if they were receiving it at home.

Listen dads, your little girls are not interested in hearing others call them princesses and queens. They want to hear those words come from your mouth and trust me when I tell you that if you don't take the time to tell them, they will search their whole life trying to find someone who will. That's why you have girls running away from home to hook up with an older guy they met online. They found someone who was willing to call them a princess and treat them like a queen.

But it's happening to our young boys as well. They are being pushed so hard in sports activities to the point that it's not even fun anymore. Dads who feel like their son is the next Michael Jordan or Stephen Curry. They sign them up for fall and summer ball so they can become the next Mark McGuire.

They push and push and push until they push their kids into thinking they are never enough. When you push like you do, you are telling your child that they are not enough the way they are. You can help them to become better by taking the pressure off from them of having to get your approval.

And let's face facts. Many of the kids on the ball fields today are simply being pushed by parents who are trying to relive their childhood. They are trying to get their kids to live out a dream they were never able to achieve.

But that is not their purpose. And they grow up thinking they are never enough for God, who is their heavenly Father because they were never enough for you who was their earthly father.

Thank God, Samuel had the boldness to check Jesse. He went

back and asked again instead of just leaving and taking a dad's word.

God doesn't make his decision about you based on what you are currently attempting to do. He chooses people he can trust to do even greater things.

Despite being looked over and not being invited to the party, David is finally brought into the home from the field. He stinks to the high heavens because he has been in the field with sheep all day. He didn't have the time clean up like his brothers did. He is coming into the house knowing that something is going on, but he is just not sure what it is.

Samuel stands before this rejected babysitter of sheep and pronounces that he is the one. He is the next king of Israel. What a moment. I am tearing up just thinking about how David must have felt. Not only did he get a major endorsement for his life, but the prophet did it in front of the boys who have been demeaning to David.

I mean David was able to be anointed for a high-ranking position in front of the dad who had forgotten about him. The dad who left him out in the field. The one who thought he was not good enough. The one who was the last choice of all his boys, yet he was God's choice the entire time.

But what do you do when you have been anointed but not yet appointed? It was Joseph Campbell who said, "We must let go of the life we have planned, so as to accept the one that is waiting for us."

David was anointed by Samuel as the next king of Israel. The only problem lies in the fact that the job is not currently open. So, what does David have to do? He simply goes back to the sheep field. After having such a moment in front of his dad and brothers, David goes right back to "babysitting" sheep. Are you kidding me? I am the next king of Israel. When it comes to the ladder of success in Israel, it doesn't get any higher up. Yet I have to go back to being the shepherd?

There's not a parade that takes place after Samuel's announcement. No one from the major news networks is calling to have an exclusive interview. Scholars tell us that David was between the ages of ten and thirteen when he was anointed king, but it wasn't until he was around the age thirty that he was appointed.

So, what do you do when you have been anointed but not yet appointed?

I know because …I am David.

At the age of sixteen years old and while traveling up and down the highway, playing my southern gospel music, God started dealing with me about another area of my life. It wasn't something I set out to do. It wasn't on my radar as something to consider for my life. I never sat in my room and dreamed about this next move. I had already made up my mind to what I was going to do with my life. I was set.

In the midst of being such a messed-up teenager, the Holy Spirit was revealing a calling on my life that God had placed there before I was ever put into my mother's womb. "Before I formed you in the womb, I knew you, before you were born, I set you apart; I appointed you as a prophet to the nations" (Jeremiah 1:5).

In those lonely moments sitting in my bedroom, listening to my gospel music, the tugging on my heart started to take place. God was revealing to me the calling upon my life to be a minister . . .

a pastor.

I was confused at first and shrugged it off the best I could. I was going to be a musician. I was going to be on the largest stages, playing in front of the largest crowds.

But moment after moment started presenting itself that would place me in a position for the Lord to speak in various situations as a way of confirmation for this calling on my life. How can this be?

In no way was I asking for this. I just wanted to be a musician and travel the world with groups I had grown up memorizing from our trade magazines. I was not looking for another church job. I was not searching out to be considered as a church speaker. I was happy and content with the current path I had created for my life.

But the feeling kept getting stronger to the point that I couldn't sleep. I finally submitted to my pastor and explained what I was dealing with. After a few more weeks of trying to forget it and leave it, it would never leave me.

So, at the age of seventeen, in between my junior and senior year of high school, I submitted my life to become a minister of the gospel of Jesus Christ.

I couldn't believe it. As messed up as I am, not fitting in, and now God has to go and cause me to make such an announcement that drives me even further away from those I am around?

It's one thing to not want Mickey, the gospel musician, coming around, but who in their right mind wants to hang around the preacher while in high school?

I AM DAVID!   Mickey Bell

While everyone else celebrated this new level of service for my life, I was back home in my bedroom, dealing with all kinds of emotions. While people were calling me to speak at their youth services and fifth quarter meetings after football games, I was struggling with the fact that God had played a bad joke on me.

You have to understand that for many people reading this book who were in my life during this time, they had no clue what I was struggling with when they were not around. I didn't tell anyone. I didn't have anyone to tell.

So, I just kept suppressing it, thinking that I could somehow outmaneuver it. While still struggling in the attempt to find my place in life, now I have to figure out what to do with this whole ministry decision. What does that even look like for a seventeen-year-old? What does a preacher do in high school? I have been raised in church all my life, so I understood how the ministry worked and the various positions that were somewhat available to me.

First of all, I knew that a church would never call a seventeen-year-old to be their pastor. I mean come on, what would your messages be like leading a church while you are still dealing with acne and girlfriends?

Churches were not looking for high school pastors just like they were not looking for high school youth ministers. So here I was again, sitting on a lonely island after coming out with this great

announcement to not understand fully what it actually meant for me. Talk about being anointed but not yet appointed. I feel ya, David. I got you, buddy. I know exactly how you feel.

I would sit at home and develop messages as though I had been doing it all my life to not have anywhere to share them. I was studying on scriptures that dealt with things I would deal with later as a pastor, but I couldn't understand why I was having to learn it at such a young age when I had nowhere to use it.

I found myself constantly watching the new twenty-four-hour Christian networks and learning about great preachers as Bishop T.D. Jakes, Rod Parsley, and E. V. Hill. I would rather watch them preach than any other show on television.

Now I am really messed up. I have so many issues that I need to deal with, but I have no outlet to get rid of it. Everyone looks at me now as though I am this well put together guy. I had never been to a movie in a theater. I have never been to a concert, other than southern gospel. I am a preacher who preaches every fifth Sunday (you will get that if you had youth Sundays at your church), but if people only knew how bad I really was.

> I am born and broken
> I have been given life from a man who left
> me. I am anointed and not yet appointed.
> I am David!

So, what do you do? Well . . . when you don't know what to do, do what you know to do! Joyce Meyer puts it this way, "Patience is not simply the ability to wait, but it's how we

behave while waiting." Sometimes God will go ahead and reveal to you what you are created to become so that when times get hard, you can rest assured that it won't kill you because God has greater plans for you.

David will end up running for his life. He will be hiding out in caves. He will have some very close calls that could take his life. But when the enemy starts causing him to doubt with those negative thoughts that you get as well, David can go back to his preteen years and recall a time when the prophet Samuel came to his village, walked in the house of his father, Jesse, and interviewed and passed on David's six older brothers. When the times get dark and discouragement starts to set in, David can remember the prophet anointing his head with oil, touching his head as a form of transferring power over to David. He can recall the moment the Spirit of the Lord came on him mightily.

I guess what I am saying is that you need these anointing moments for when you need a flashback in your life. Because life is going to get hard, times are going to get tough, and you will need a reminder of the purpose God has for you.

A flashback will give you shouting moments in the middle of your loneliness. You have your own worship service in the unemployment line. You can be cleaning up your house, knowing that one day someone else will be cleaning it for you. (Come on and shout somebody.)

It's good for our own motivation to get a flashback to see where God has brought us from, but I am also thankful for the moment when God will take me back to remind me where he is taking me.

You are blessed far beyond your current bank balance. You are blessed far beyond the job you currently hold. Pastor, you are

blessed far beyond the seats that are being taken up on Sundays. Blessed beyond what your checkbook says, blessed beyond what others might say.

Come on, David, don't focus on what you don't have . . . yet! You might be overseeing a sheep field today, but you will soon be overseeing an entire nation. Today you might only have sheep following you, but soon an entire nation will be following your lead.

I AM DAVID!

Mickey Bell

They may call you a little shepherd boy today, but soon they will call you *king*! Keep holding on. Keep your focus right. Don't give up; don't give in. What God has for you is far greater than what you can get for yourself. Your anointing time has come, and your appointing time is just around the corner.

CHAPTER 6
Talents and Transitions

The Lord removed his hand from Saul simply because Saul decided he didn't need the Lord anymore. He started making his own decisions and taking credit for the "wins" in his life (1 Samuel 15:23).

After David was anointed as the new king, it's now time for the process of transition to take place. God started shaking Saul to the point that he was losing his mind. The Bible says in 1 Samuel 16:14 that the Spirit of the Lord had been replaced with an evil spirit that is now terrorizing the King: "Now the Spirit of the Lord had departed from Saul, and an evil spirit from the Lord tormented him."

The only thing that would calm down Saul was the beautiful playing of the harp. So, the servants of Saul were instructed to find a musician who could come inside the kingdom to play for the king whenever he was shaken.

Well, it just so happened that David was not only a shepherd boy, but also a musician. Word had spread around town in how talented David was on the harp so much so, that the king requested his presence. Did you see that? It was the talent of the musician that put the new king inside the kingdom for the transition of power. That is so good!

David's musical instrument was called the *kinnor*, which we usually translate as a lyre, or harp. It probably had ten strings.

I AM DAVID!

Mickey Bell

Each string played a different note on what is called the *pentatonic* (five note) scale. It made a soft, sweet sound.

All those times David was in the field playing his harp for a crowd of stinky sheep, he was simply practicing for when he got called up to the big stage. While God has bigger and better plans for David, he was using his love for music to get him to the place in which he would serve. Out of all the musicians who could have been selected, David got the call. Out of all the people in the land that could play the harp, David was the one chosen. Do you see how his anointing is starting to open the doors in preparation for his time of appointing?

I understand this simply because . . . I AM DAVID.

Upon graduating high school, I am now trying to decide what I want to be when I grow up. All through elementary and junior high school, it was well known that I had plans of traveling the world as a musician. Not just any musician, but a southern gospel musician. That world was so much bigger back then.

For the next several years (just like David), I used my talents as a musician in many different capacities. I was able to see my dreams become a reality by being asked to travel with several groups that are still known in the industry today.

Oh, the feeling of being able to crawl into a bus and ride down the highway. Getting into my bunk every night and becoming that ten-year-old boy again. Thinking back to those moments I used to lie awake, dreaming and praying for this to actually happen.

It started on a regional scale with a group known as New Ground. These friends from Scottsboro, Alabama, became like family to me because we were able to experience a lot of things together. From recording our first national project, to opening for many of the groups I found myself looking up to as a kid.

They gave me my first experience in a Nashville recording session. Watching as a song went from words on a sheet of paper to a full-blown musical composition recorded by the best. This was my first step inside the workings of the industry.

I would soon be able to travel with the Steeles, as well as, Tony Gore and Majesty. With both of these groups, I was able to experience having number-one songs in the charts and being with new artists who were in great demand. I suffered with eight-hour trips in a van when the bus was broke down. I endured five-hour trips one way, just to meet up with the bus to go out for the weekend.

My final full-time tour would come with a legendary group known as the Nelons. With this group, I was able to appear on the magazine covers, travel the world, and work with the Gaither Homecoming tours, but more importantly, I was able to spend time talking with one of the greatest statesmen of this industry. Rex Nelon was one of the great ones who would get overlooked when people are making their list of great icons of our genre.

Oh, to be able to go back and listen to his stories of the good ole' days and learn the tricks of the trade when it comes to publishing and managing a group. To hear his humorous stories about being on the road and hearing how they use to "rough it", just to be able to sing. A lot of great experiences and certainly a lot of great memories.

During the course of my time playing music full-time, I was able to participate with groups that I used to read about in the trade magazines. The "big" concerts that were talked about on various pages had now become a page in my memory as being able to say that I have done it.

Being on the cover of magazines that I once memorized, to

playing on convention stages and cruise lines. I was able to travel with multiple groups who experienced number one songs, and I have been on the bus with those who are regarded as some of the "heroes" of our industry.

I have been able to see much of the United States because of my music. Playing golf in Colorado, eating lunch in the Space Needle, and being nominated for Doves and Grammy Awards.

I was actually able to attend my first movie at a movie theater while traveling. I was able see *The Preacher's Wife* with Whitney Houston. Awesome! I had to call home and confess to my Independent Baptist parents. LOL!

It was surreal to come off stage and be greeted by young people who have the same desire to be in this industry just as I did when I was their age. Being able to sign their pictures and give them a word of encouragement about not giving up on their dreams.

What a life I was able to live during this time. There wasn't a lot of money in this industry, but that was okay because the people who are doing this type of music know going into it that you are not going to be rich, or if they do think that, they find out rather quickly.

I also learned that the spotlight is not all what it is cracked up to be when the light is turned out. Just because you have the word Christian in your songs or in your profile doesn't always mean that everyone who is on stage is an actual believer. That was hard for me to digest as a young person coming into this industry. I always assumed this would be a safe place for a young person to be.

While many artists encouraged me along the way, I was never

given a heads-up about the backbiting and competition that existed. But before you judge this industry for that, you might want to look under your church pews because it exists there as well... If not more!

I have been backstage, where other musicians would "bully" me in various situations. I have seen promoters and artists almost come to blows over money and stage time. I have stood and watched as artists in the same field tear each other apart with rumors and gossips. You can put the label of Christian on anything from music to churches, but the moment you get imperfect people involved, you have a mess.

My dream of traveling only lasted a few years. While I was thankful for all I was able to accomplish and experience, the inner demons were pushing me in all different directions, and I became very confused and disoriented about what to do with my life.

During this time, I started to become even more insecure about who I was and what was about to come before me. I started realizing the problem I had with abandonment. And just because I never talked about it, doesn't mean it stayed away.

One illustration that I am ashamed to admit, proves how insecure I was with my own life. If I ever got a girlfriend and we started to become serious with our relationship, I started moving quickly toward the subject of marriage. I would quickly buy a ring out of desperation of wanting to get her committed so she wouldn't leave me. I thought marriage meant that she would never leave me or cheat on me.

Everyone around just saw a strange guy who couldn't make up his mind, but I was actually fighting demons who were constantly telling me how many people were going to leave me by myself. It was bad. I was allowing my insecurities to mess up

the lives of girls who thought I really loved them enough to marry them.

I was so ashamed, which then just added another level of mistrust I had for myself. Another level of insecurity about being able to find the right one without making the decision based on my inner demons instead of being in love with that person.

My heart has been broken many times. Not only by others, but from the decisions I made myself. I could feel the laughter of people when they would approach me. I could sense their judgment when they asked about me. I may have been in my early twenties at this time, but I was still the thirteen-year-old boy who was dealing with his own dad walking out of his life.

Talk about a whirlwind. I was making so many mistakes in the decisions I was making. It had nothing to do with vices, such as drugs, alcohol, or even sex. It had everything to do with me trying to figure out who I was. Trying to see who God wanted me to be, but also trying to become that person that no one would want to leave.

I just wanted to be able to find a person that would love me in spite of me. I was so ready to become the person God created me to be, but I felt like I was a million miles away from accomplishing that goal.

But it would be my music and the talents I had on stage that would create a profile that surrounded Mickey Bell. This was what I was known for. I met many pastors and church leaders simply because of the concerts and events we would do at various churches.

It would be these connections that would benefit me later in life when the ministry positions started calling. it's frustrating when

you have the anointing to serve, but you are having to watch other people who are in your position.

I can remember after coming off the road of just wanting pastors to call me to preach. Just to be called to do a revival meeting or fill in for them one weekend. Do you know what it's like to have the anointing but not the appointing? David does because he was a very young man when his life was prophesied by the prophet Samuel, and it would be his talents of music and songwriting that would carry him from the field to the palace.

The musician would play his way from the outside of the kingdom to the inside. God is sneaky sometimes! When there seems to be no way of getting you in, God creates a way to where you are not only talented to do the job, but you become the one in demand.

David was being used for his talents to benefit the king. But while he may have just considered himself a musician, he was at least inside the kingdom that would one day belong to him.

Don't discount the talents you have in your possession. They may not be what gets you the position, but they could be what opens the door. God has placed inside of you everything you need to accomplish, and everything you desire. Not one talent was wasted on you. Who would have thought that a chicken sandwich could provide more than $45 million dollars in college scholarship money? That is what has happened when Chick-fil-A owner, Truett Cathy, set out to invest into the future of his employees.

Work with your talents. Do what you enjoy doing.

Don't wait to get a paycheck before you start displaying talent.

It may just be your talent that opens up the door.

David was anointed as king, but here he is having to take orders from the king. He was anointed for the position that is now telling him what to do, and when to do it. But that's okay because David was so much closer to his destiny than he realized. I know because ... I AM DAVID!

CHAPTER 7
Is it Real or is it
Just Me Again?

After coming off the road of my dreams, I started searching for people and careers that would make me happy. Those decisions took me from being a business owner of a Christian bookstore to becoming a financial adviser. It was during this time of my life I found myself working for a financial institution near my hometown. I had arrived at this point in my life, heartbroken and confused about my future. At this time, I wasn't looking for a career, but rather just a place to bide my time that would help me make my truck payment each month.

I was not only looking for a job, I was looking for myself. I was lost in this big world and trying to figure out who I was. This thought kept ringing in my ear, "What do you do when you have accomplished all you set out to do in life, and you're only twenty-three years old?" That was where I was at in life. I was in my early twenties with no ambition.

I was okay at the jobs I took because the people knew me in my hometown. I had been playing music in their churches since I was ten years old. I had sold them Bibles as they came into my bookstore. So, dealing with the public wasn't a problem for me, but I still went home each night asking the question, "Why am I here?"

Day after day, I was just clocking in and clocking out, feeling like at twenty-three years old, I was losing control of my life. I felt like I was wasting time, as well as, dealing with my inner emotions. I was miserable, and I was looking for anything that could make things better.

I was looking for dates. I was looking for friends. I was looking for a career. I was looking for relief, but I just didn't know how to find it. I wanted so bad to be well, but I didn't even know what that looked or felt like. I wanted to talk to someone about my inner demons, but that wasn't something we did in our home. The thought of counselors was looked at as a weakness or lack of faith in God. We were of the belief, that as long as you were a believer in Christ, went to church all the time, then everything else would work itself out.

Well, it wasn't, and I didn't know what to do.

One day in March, my boss decided she was going to fix me up. She was tired of me feeling sorry for myself, and I think she was tired of all the girls coming into the office. So, she sent me to another branch connected with our institution to "deliver some very important papers." The only catch was, that I had to take out the girl up front for lunch.

At this point, I didn't even care. It was a day out of the office, and I wasn't being told how late to stay out. So, I drove the forty minutes to the other office. Just to show how messed up I was, I wasn't even nervous. I got out of my car, walked straight into the office, and yelled out, "Who am I taking to lunch?"

That is when my eyes fell on Wendy Jones. Long, natural curly hair, with a smile that would melt ice cream. This was by no means love at first sight for either one of us. In fact, she would tell you that she was only interested in the free meal and time away from the office. She was hoping I was just in and out for the day.

I AM DAVID!

Mickey Bell

Off to lunch, we went just talking about our business connections and the various office drama and gossip. I really don't remember much about that conversation instead of the fact that it was very enjoyable, and I felt comfortable. Not comfortable enough to open up, but just enough to make it through the date without getting sick. All I wanted to do was make it through this lunch without showing any of my downfalls or coming across as needy. I hear that is not very attractive.

I had a great plan for this date. I was going to impress her with my credentials as a southern gospel musician. She was not impressed.

In fact, she had no clue what type of music I was talking about, nor did she know any groups in the industry.

Well, that's a wrap. That's all I had to offer.

I almost made it through the entire date without being my normal idiot self until the moment I was walking her back to the car. As I opened up the door for her to get inside, the words just slipped out. I didn't really mean them, and it was meant as a joke. But I looked at her and said, "So when are we getting married?"

Are you kidding me?

This was our first date. I was not in love with her. She was definitely not in love with me. The only thing she enjoyed about the date was that I paid for lunch, and my cute butt! I found that out later. He he he.

We laughed off my moment of insecurity, and I drove her back to her office. All the way home, I couldn't get rid of the feeling of wanting to see her again. She was different than the other girls I had dated. She wasn't trying to impress me, and she had this "I don't care" attitude that was weirdly refreshing.

She wasn't out with the musician.
She wasn't out with the preacher.
She wasn't out with what others had perceived.
She simply didn't care, and I loved it.

When I got back to my office, I started using our inner office messaging system, because we did not have text messages back in that day. I was sending her all kinds of messages to convince her to see me again that night. That was a very enlightening day. That was when I found out that every employee of every office in the three states was able to read all my messages.

Yep. Every employee of this company was able to witness the grappling I did on that day to convince this girl to see me again. They also witnessed every comeback she had to my flirtatious comments.

Oh well . . . it worked because I got her to commit to seeing me again. She tried her best to come up with every reason on why she couldn't see me that night, but my delightful charm won her over. (She is laughing right now for sure.)

Days turned into weeks, and weeks turned into months. Her family was even shocked that she was even giving me the time of day. I think they actually had a bet on how long I would be around. I was the total opposite of what she would date. She liked the "bad boys" who gets into a lot of trouble. You should have seen her mom's face when she showed up with the *preacher boy*. That was the term that I would hear a lot in that household when they were referring to me.

She was into horses and was currently in the phase of wanting to date cowboys. Well, I was a lot of things, and a cowboy was definitely not one of them. Her perfect guy would be the bull rider who would accompany her to weekend rodeos as she became the barrel racing champion.

I got tangled up with a horse one time and almost died. If the manager of K-Mart hadn't come out and unplugged it when he did, I would not be here to share my testimony with you. That's bad I know, but that accurately describes how far I was at being who she wanted me to be.

It wasn't long before my insecurities and inner demons started kicking in. The more time we spent together, the more attached I was getting to the notion of having someone in my life again. And once again, wouldn't you know it, I am pushing for a much deeper commitment when neither one of us was truly ready for it.

I was nothing compared to what she was looking for. I was simply looking for anyone that was breathing that would show me some attention. And wouldn't you know it, within months, we were engaged. We both agreed that it was one of the most ridiculous decisions we ever made. We were not in love. We were not even wanting to spend the rest of our lives together.

This book is not to deal with the life of Wendy, but we have been able to admit to each other that she was trying to deal with some things in her own life. That was the reason she committed so quickly. To her, I was a way of escape. She saw me as a way out of the house that caused her to feel like a prisoner. So here we are, two newlyweds who were not in love with each other, but we got married to offset the demons we were fighting from our past. Oh, this should be fun! This is the perfect setup for a happy ending.

Her background did not match at all with mine. I came from a very strict family who kept tight reins on me. She was sowing her oats and enjoying every minute of it. For her, the new husband in her life was nothing but a kill joy. Every time she wanted to go out and have fun, I was standing in the doorway with my King James Bible telling her that I didn't want her going to hell. I was shouting out, "Thou shalt not" and she was replying, "Oh hell I will . . ." We couldn't go to other wedding ceremonies because I thought if they were serving alcohol that I would go to hell for just being in attendance, and then she would want me to dance with her. What? I can't dance; I'm Independent Baptist.

I can admit to you now that we were miserable. Something her family didn't know, and my family surely didn't know was that we both wanted out. My insecurities were too difficult to live with, and her desire to be with me so she could live free was not what she had in mind. While I didn't want her to leave me because of my abandonment issues, she was ready to walk out the door, and I really didn't blame her. But then something happened. It wasn't a spiritual moment that we can both relate to. She was pregnant. Oh crap! What do we do now?

I would love to say that things got better when we brought Brindley Logan Bell into this world. While we had better days, this was more pressure on our relationship that we thought was never created to be strong enough to handle all our issues. For the next several years, we scraped to make ends meet. We look back on those days and know that it had to be God that helped us make it through those years of financial struggle, and it was my fault. I was so uncommitted to anything because I was dealing with so much confusion and hurt that I didn't really know what I wanted to do.

This was not the dream I had as a ten-year-old boy memorizing trade magazines for gospel music. I didn't know what I wanted to do as a career. I just simply knew I didn't want to be alone and I had a demon reminding me of that every day. So here

I would go, jumping from job to job, causing us to get further in debt, which was not good for any couple, much less one that was not stable.

I was not happy with any place that I worked because it wasn't my purpose, but I was so screwed up in the head that I couldn't define what my purpose was in life, much less able to find it.

Then came the moment things got . . . worse! Wendy and I were not able to talk to each other and be with the other without a problem. I still don't think we were in love with each other. We were just making do with the situation that was before us.

Keep in mind that during all this struggle and fighting, she knows nothing about what I am dealing with on the inside. She knows I am messed up because of my actions, but she doesn't realize how bad off I really am...nor was I willing to tell her. So, the inner fighting continued inside of me. I was in torment. I was miserable. I didn't know how to handle it, and I was making her life miser- able because who wants to live with a demon?

It was during this time I started having private online conversations with other women. I thought it was innocent in how it started. I would simply hide behind a screen and share information that I couldn't share with anyone face-to-face, or that is what I was telling myself. I would mention my difficult marriage, and they were more than willing to soothe it over by talking to me.

Once Wendy found out about these messages, our marriage was

at a major fork in the road. She had already spent Thanksgiving away from me, and I was spiraling down a deep hole because I

didn't know how I could handle her walking out of my life, and now walking out with my daughter in hand.

We decided to take a trip to a bed and breakfast in Tennessee just outside of Nashville. I remember the drive and how cold it was. Not on the outside, but on the inside of the car. From Huntsville to Nashville, we didn't say two words to each other. I was preparing myself mentally for what I thought was about to happen. My worst fears were about to play right out before my eyes.

While the trip afforded us the opportunity to talk things through our current storm, I was still unable to tell her everything. I am not sure what all happened on that trip, but I started looking at Wendy in a different light. I really think it's because she didn't leave me. I gave her reasons to leave, but she stayed to work it out. While I was relieved that she wasn't leaving me, there was a battle still raging inside of me that would not stop.

Things seem to get a bit better for us. I was somewhat moving back toward a prayer life and finding God again. During this time of our lives, I was nowhere near the presence of God. As I began to rededicate myself, doors started opening for me to minister. I was going and playing the piano and sharing only parts of my testimony that I was able to share.

One day, the phone rang, and it was a bit bizarre. It was the pastor of a church where I grew up as a child. His words were a bit confusing when he said, "We want you to come lead our music." In fact, they had already voted me in without asking if I was even interested.

Coming from my upbringing around church, I was open to the

new road in our life, but Wendy was having none of it. I don't blame her. Our marriage was a mess, and now we were going to

move ourselves into the glass house that ministers and church staff have to live in? She not only said no; she said, "Hell no!"

I decided to not say anything else about it, and simply pray over the situation. A few weeks later, Wendy came to me and suggested we just take some time together as a family. We didn't have the money to go anywhere, so we just went for a drive. A drive that would have us ending up in the city of the church that had reached out to us.

When we arrived at the area, we passed by the church, and I noticed she started asking questions about the position. A few moments later, we were sitting in the driveway of the house the church was going to let us live in while we served them.

Up until this point, Wendy never wanted to talk about this ministry opportunity as an option, but on this day, she was interested in seeing the house. I called the pastor, and he came to give us a tour. While we walked from room to room, I started listening to my wife as she started telling me where we could place what little furniture we owned, and right there before my eyes, God started placing the two of us in ministry together. Wow! What a sight. We were nowhere ready to do this. We were in no way mentally, emotionally, or spiritually ready . . . but God opened the door anyway.

During our time there, we were able to serve in the capacity of music and youth. We both fell in love with our teens and became a part of their lives that still enrich us today. It's weird to see them getting married and having kids of their own. In our eyes, they should still be in the sixth and seventh grade, playing hide-and-seek throughout the entire community. What I would give to go back to those days!

From the young age in which David was anointed as king of Israel until the day he was appointed, there were a lot of ups

and downs. He didn't always make the right decisions. He wasn't always faithful to his calling, but he kept pressing onward.

Just like David, I found myself being used by God even though I wasn't worthy to be used. We were reaching teens for Christ while we are still messed up inside. I think Wendy and I were both hoping that our lives were growing closer together.

But there is something that is keeping us from that . . .

I AM DAVID.

CHAPTER 8
Pastor with a Past

You can continue to walk through the scriptures of 1 Samuel and see how David made his way from the musician of the kingdom to the king. He went from the harp to the king's throne. When you view his journey as a complete piece, you will see that he had a lot of twists and turns. He made some good decisions, but he also made some bad decisions. He was committed in some areas of his life, and then other times, well, he was just completely messed up. He had some of the most unlikely people in his life that he could trust, yet he had some people who were after him because not everyone wanted to see David on the throne.

Before he made it to the kingdom, we have a moment in the life of David that made him the most popular. We have seen him being sent to the battleground where his brothers were stationed for battle. While there, his moment of opportunity came, and he was able to come face-to-face with Goliath. A victory that set the course of advancement for this young shepherd boy.

With this win came a lot of great bonuses and recognition, but not every attention that is drawn to you is good for you. While the attention of some was bringing praise to David, it was the spotlight of this massive win that brought the pain of David having to keep away from Saul.

I AM DAVID!

Mickey Bell

Wow! What a statement.

Not every attention that is drawn to you is good for you. I know this because . . . I AM DAVID.

Upon graduating from the ranks of youth and music ministry, I felt the call to advance my ministry to another level. I sensed God was leading me to become a pastor and to serve as a leader for a small congregation. It was at this time in my life, that my family submitted to the call of a small Baptist church in Madison County.

I am nowhere healed from my own demons, but I truly felt God leading and opening this door for us. The moment we began this chapter of our lives was the moment God's blessing was on the church. We were seeing a great number of people commit their life to Christ. We were baptizing people left and right. We were seeing families restored and many people coming back to church who had fallen away.

While serving as pastor of this church, we were also able to get the church debt-free and set in motion a foundation for which a great work could be accomplished, but then the enemy inside of me rose up again.

While seeing so many come in, the devil began to stir as well, and I had to deal with the thought of some families leaving. Of course, after reading up until this point, you can imagine what this does to a man who has been dealing with these types of issues all my life.

I am not good with people leaving me. In fact, this is the reason I am so messed up at this point in my life because it started with a very important figure walking out on me, and since I have never been able to correctly deal with these demons, I am now full of abandonment issues which is not a great quality to put on your resumé when you want to become the next pastor of a great church.

My first church to pastor was coming off a hurtful split. The people were in pain. The staff was in pain. Heck, the pastor they were bringing in was in pain. They just didn't know it at the moment, and to be truthful, I didn't realize at the time that my pain was as important as I see now. This is something I have had to deal with all my life, and God has continued to open doors and bless the things I touch. So why should I have questioned if I was capable of leading a congregation while bleeding on the inside myself?

While serving in this church, my demons began to work me over. I was always nervous of people leaving. I was constantly working overtime, trying to keep everyone happy. By the way, have you ever tried to keep everyone in the church happy at the same time? It's impossible, but I was giving it all I had to the point of exhaustion and bad decisions.

One in particular was a repeat of what had happened to me in the past. I got too close to a female and began sending text messages that should have never been sent. It was at a moment in my life when I would feel alone and nervous about being left all alone. I am not making any excuses, just giving you my thought process at the time.

I stood and admitted to the church what had happened. They were so loving and forgiving. In fact, they wanted me to stay on as pastor even though I had failed them. They understood the means of restoration and forgiveness. I was blown away with their compassion, but the challenge from hell came up on this situation. The devil had his own workers inside the church that he wanted to be in charge, so the mess began. Accusations that were not true. Stories told that never happened. All made-up lies to accompany what I had admitted that I did do. Just know that you have many people sitting at the table with you, and one could very well be Judas.

The best thing to do for my family and the church was leave. That was one of the most miserable times of my life when it comes to ministry. I thought I had done right by coming forward to the church. All while trying to save the church and the loving people who were there, I never took the time to try to fix me.

The pain was just too great. The embarrassment was just too questionable. So again, I kept it all to myself and suppressed even more baggage to my life. After some time away from church, I submitted to a local pastor who ministered to me in my time of need, but he could only help what I was willing to bring to the surface. So instead of dealing with all the pain from my past, we only dealt with the pain from the church situation. So, to no fault of his own, he did what he could do, and I appreciate him for that. I remember leaving his office only to feel a heaviness for the fact that I couldn't completely open up to him.

What would he think?

Would he tell me my ministry was done? Would he lose all respect for me?

This was my purpose for being born. I don't know what I would do if I couldn't preach and minister. I couldn't take that chance. So out of fear that I was too messed up to be a pastor, I just kept it all to myself and struggled to move forward.

As time went by, it got a bit easier to live. I was getting back to the place where I could breathe again. With Wendy still by my side, we kept plugging along by going from one church to the next, preaching for them and appreciating every opportunity God gave us to do it. During this time in our lives, we met so many great, loving people who loved on my family as though we were a part of their own. I have been able to meet some very

special people in my life.

I was opening up the best I could to share with these people what I was experiencing. I wouldn't share everything, but I noticed God was blessing what I was able to share, and we were able to see lives changed.

Then came the day when our next church would reach out to us to start the conversation of us making a major move in our life. Up until this point, Wendy and I have always lived within an hour distance from both of our families, but this new endeavor would require us to move two hours away.

After discussing it in depth, we were looking forward to starting this new chapter in our lives. I was looking forward to getting away from people who knew me. I thought getting away would be the perfect solution to handling the emotional wreck I am on the inside. We came into our new work with great excitement and anticipation. Just as before, God began blessing the work, and lives were being changed. During this time, Wendy and I seemed to be getting closer to each other, because this new work just made a lot of things easier in our life. We had a great house, a good salary, and opportunity for great growth. Everything around seemed to be changing for the better, except . . . me. Why? because . . . I AM DAVID.

I look back now and see another demon effect in my life that I never recognized before. In fact, I didn't recognize it until recently, but it was there all the time. In her book *The Healing Creed*, Becky Dvorak explained it in such a way that made so much sense to me. Here's how she put it:

> Can we lay aside the spirit of pride and the sin of entitlement? Does the spotlight have to always shine on us? Are we content to being one of his servants?
> Or do we feel the need to be "the Servant."?

Oh my. I never saw this before in my life. I never saw this tight grip that had a hold of me.

Earlier I shared with you that I could be in front of thousands as long as I was in the spotlight. That fed my ego. That gave the affirmation that was lacking in my life, but what I didn't realize was how the enemy was using this against me.

I couldn't just be a pastor; I had to be *the* best pastor. I couldn't just pastor a great church; I had to pastor *the* best church in the community. I wanted all the attention that I could get, simply because I was feeding a demon inside of me that was never getting full.

Being on stage, preaching with everyone's attention, was no different at thirty or forty as it was when I was only ten playing music. Just as the stage back then was my safe place, it still works for me now. When I was on stage, no one cares how tall I am or what I look like compared to others. I am in a place where I can demand your attention. I can make you laugh, cry, and think. I am in control even to the point of falling into the sin trap of entitlement.

Let me go out on a limb here and suggest that I am not the only pastor who deals with this particular sin. You can't go to a preacher's meeting without someone asking you how many you ran this past Sunday. They don't care how many people were saved; they just want to see where they measure up against you. I was serving as pastor in a denomination much like all the others where they would mail you the annual report. I assume it was the same for every pastor who seeks to be declared a success.

We would first go and look up our church to ensure the numbers

were correct. The pages would then begin to turn to locate the church name that we are in competition with down the street.

How much offerings did they bring in this year? What was their worship attendance? Did they have any baptisms this year? It's as though one sin leads to another because if not checked, our sin of entitlement will then take us back to when were young teens comparing ourselves to others in our class, and we say we have grown up!

This is a grip that will cause you to live a miserable life if not dealt with. The spirit of entitlement will have you thinking that no one in the church can preach, but you. It will have you dictating every move. It will cause you to believe the lie that you are the only one who can lead people to Christ.

This is a very scary place to be when you think the church revolves around you. That's why many pastors are scared to take a vacation. We are taught at every conference the importance of getting away to rest. Those smarter than us, attempts to convince us that we must step away or we will burn out.

On those occasions when we finally convince ourselves that we have to have a vacation day that includes a Sunday morning, we will bring in a guy who we feel can't preach as well as us because we can't be outdone while we are gone. Forget the fact, our congregation needs a word; just don't want to be replaced. So, we secretly hope attendance is down. We feed off the comments of how much they missed us. The sin of entitlement.

When I read the above statement from Becky's book, I had to throw the book down. It was like being shocked by an electric fence. There was no way I could proceed until I dealt with my sin of entitlement. Again, I am just coming to terms with this five-year removed from this church situation, but I look back and see where this demonic force was affecting me then.

That was me! I was the pastor who checked the annual reports. I

was the pastor that felt like the entire community should come to *my* church. I was the pastor who wanted to be considered better than all the others. Now couple the demon of abandonment with the demon of entitlement, and you have me. How would you like to be on the pas tor search committee and see that on a resumé? Since I am still operating out of pain, hurt, abandonment, and regret while everything on the outside is going great, the demons on the inside of me are tormenting me to the point of not having any emotion. I am not running on the love of Christ, but the spirit of competition and entitlement.

People tried to love on me and my family, but I wouldn't let them into my head or into my past. I was able to mention some of my issues during my messages in hopes that it would make me feel better about myself, but I always kept people at an arm's distance. Well, except the wrong people.

While everything was booming, the spotlight on our ministry was getting stronger, and I was feeding my need to be "the one." It was attracting a lot of people with various opportunities. I was being asked to preach in various churches, and I was featured on a weekly television show that aired every Sunday.

Preachers were reaching out to me. Churches were booking me to preach their revivals. People were recognizing me everywhere I went in the community. I was a hot mess on the road, creating an even hotter mess. While the spotlight draws attention, it also attracts the insects. Those bugs that come to suck the life right out of you. They are in every church.

I AM DAVID!

Mickey Bell

These are people who are connected to you all for the wrong reasons. They want to have your attention, but only for their benefit. Their lives may be miserable, so they want to live a life

through you, and when you have a history such as I have, I welcomed the attention. Even though it was the wrong attention.

Once again, Wendy found text messages that were close to crossing the line, and many that did until the day when I allowed myself to be overtaken with emotion and regret. I was in a battle that no one could help me with simply because I wouldn't open up for help. It caused me to make a decision that would forever haunt me for the rest of my life. I can still hear the demons rejoicing over my fall. I can still remember the emptiness that I felt inside of me. It wasn't until four years later that my sin would come to light.

I had been able to put it so far back that I didn't think anyone would ever find it, and while those who found my skeleton were rejoicing over their find . . . My world was turned upside down.

David made the same mistake when he took Bathsheba into his bedroom. She became pregnant, and the child was born sick. While the child was fighting for his life, now King David was found on the floor pleading with God for the sick child. I found myself reading and studying the life of David simply because I finally found someone who I could relate to because . . . I am David.

Several times, I considered ending my life for the sake of making all this torment stop inside of me. You would think that these actions from those who hated me would have pushed me to the point of wanting to be set free, but it didn't. It wasn't because I didn't want to be set free, but I didn't know how.

To be set free from what was tormenting me meant I had to come to terms with the action in how these demons were put into place to affect me. I couldn't stop doing what I was doing. The harder I tried, the worse I became. That is because of

another demon that had control over me. I didn't really understand until I started reaching out for answers, but I was too ashamed to ask the real questions that would give me the

life-changing answers that I needed. This is part of the testimony that I haven't been able to share, until now.

My mom and dad were hard working people. They made sure my brother and sisters were taken care of even if that meant they had to leave us with sitters throughout the day. While they did not know, I dreaded going to some of the homes in which I had to stay, mainly because of what would happen to me after my parents would leave.

At a very young age, I had cousins that were inappropriately touching me and doing things to me that should only be done after a ceremony of marriage. I was unable to share this with anyone. I felt dirty and ashamed, but I couldn't tell anyone. Most people would consider my upbringing to be stricter than most and maybe not as strict as some. This information would have crushed our family. So, I bought into the lie that I had to remain silent.

This is also the lie the enemy has used to keep you bound. You feel isolated and backed up in a corner. When you look around, you see people who say they love you, but you don't see anyone that you can trust with the information that you are hiding. It's not that you don't want to tell someone; you are just afraid of telling the wrong someone. I get it!

It was at this moment in my life that a demon of sexual

perversion was developed inside of me that I would have a hard time dealing with for the next thirty-plus years, because anything left alone will not just go away, but rather will keep growing. It's like a root that never goes away. You can't just wish

it away, and you can't just keep hiding it, because it keeps growing until the point it becomes bigger than you can handle.

As I would get older, this demon would show himself with things such as porn and text messages. The grip that was on me was so

strong that I couldn't break it. I don't know what it's like to be addicted to drugs, alcohol, or even tobacco, but I know what this addiction was like... It was suffocating.

It was constantly on my mind. I couldn't get away from it.

You must first admit to yourself; this demon is just as real as the demon that has you addicted to painkillers, cigarettes, and caffeine drinks. The same grip that has a hold of you had a hold of me, and I couldn't make it let go. I didn't know how to make it go away.

All my life, I was subject to this control. I couldn't defeat it. I couldn't stay clear of it. It would follow me everywhere I go and just added another level of control that was already placed upon my life. It didn't care that I was a husband and a father. It didn't care that I was a pastor of a growing church. What did I do to deserve this?

Many of the struggles that adults face today have nothing to do with the decisions you have made. They have everything to do with what someone else has placed on you or within you. Their decisions have caused you to develop the strongholds that you can't break.

If you are not brought up in the ways of the Word in knowing how to speak against these forces within you, then you will live your life completely exposed to their control. That was me. I knew about the love of Christ for me. I knew all the wrong things we were not supposed to do, but no one ever told me

how to get rid of the demons that controlled me. I had God's Word that I could read for myself, but I stayed in the areas that made me feel good.

If you are someone who doesn't believe that you can be con-

trolled by an outside source, then tell me why you can't quit some of the things you do? Why is that you can't quit smoking without patches or special gum? Why is that you have to have that first cup of coffee and then three others throughout the day?

Why is it that a drug addict has to commit to a twelve-step program and live the rest of his life on high alert of triggers? Because he is entertaining a control on the inside. You can preach that a person should just get saved, but just because you are saved doesn't mean you will forever be removed from the temptation to sin.

The Apostle Paul says I have to choose each day whether to walk by the Spirit or by the flesh. Just because I am delivered doesn't mean the temptations will stop. Why are you unable to put the bottle down? You have told yourself a hundred times over that you would never go back to it to only find yourself on Monday hungover once again. Are you just making bad decisions, or are you being controlled by a force (a demon) that you are unable to tame?

The demon of abandonment.

I AM DAVID!

Mickey Bell

The demon of entitlement.

The demon of sexual perversion.

There it is. In black and white for the entire world to see. The

source of my struggle put out in front of you. So, what are you struggling with? The problem with our religious institutions of today is we want to be selective as to who can come clean. Let a family member admit their issues to get help, and we will praise them even if they are a deacon of a church.

Let your pastor admit his issues, and we fire him on the spot. I

understand. I get it. That's why some of the pastors reading these words right now are shaking under conviction because while you are holding this book, there is a power that has a hold of you. You can't afford to tell anyone for the chance of losing your job. You live in church housing; you would be evicted without notice. So here you sit with a secret that you are unable to share with anyone.

What are you going to do?

You have had some close calls. There have been moments where you were almost exposed. Times in your life when you almost lost it all, but you were able to keep it all together . . . this time.

But do you trust yourself? Can you be left alone at home with just you and a computer? Can you go out by yourself and not be threatened with the temptations of your past?

Coming from a pastor who had to learn this in the public eye, read the following words carefully: There is a way out! There is freedom!

You don't have to continue to live in this condition. When Christ said that he came so you could have life and have it more abundantly, that meant demon-free. That meant you could live without the strongholds in your life, but you must take action to get free.

The stronger the hold that is on you, the stronger the fight you will have to get rid of it. The longer you wait, the stronger Satan's grip is on your life. Kick him out! Let's make the decision that he is no longer going to control you.

"Confess your sins one to another" (James 5:16). Every guy

needs one. Every woman needs one as well. We all need that special someone in our life that we can be totally honest with. A person who can know the real you and not run away. They are hard to find these days.

In a world where we are fueled on gossip and rumors, we have this innate goal to be the person in the know, so the juicier the information we can find, the bigger we think it makes us when we share it.

Just because this individual is hard for you to find doesn't excuse you from the search. There is a good reason why God told us to confess our sins one to another.

I don't think his thoughts were for us to stand and announce our sins to the entire community. I don't suggest creating a social media page dedicated to airing out every sin you commit, but I do feel it is important for you to have someone in which you can be totally honest with.

This confession to another person is not for the means of

forgiveness, but for healing. There is something that takes place when you are able to verbally communicate your weaknesses and shortcomings.

Somewhere we have turned this around backward. Instead of being churches where the "sin sick" people can come to get well, we have polished our furniture and created an atmosphere

of perfection. It's almost like we are saying you have to be totally clean before you can attend our churches. We don't care if you come, just don't get your nastiness on our pews. We just got them cleaned last week.

In our effort to create the "perfect" church that we think God would be proud to visit, we have polished ourselves so clean on the outside that we have turned more people away because

they don't feel like they measure up to your standards.

Thus, creating the mindset that I can't tell anyone about my sin, or they will kick me out. You do realize that you can polish the furniture inside the church, but you still have nasty people attending. But again, I get it, you have trained them to put on the mask of perfection even though their lives are a long way from it.

These types of scenarios in our church houses today are defeating the purpose God had in our worship services. We think he is attracted to our modern, contemporary worship style with lights and smoke. We have this idea, if we turn it up loud and keep it dark, then the Almighty will show up. We need everyone standing because God doesn't like for you to sit. We need everyone singing, or he won't show up, so we will put the words on the screen. To   make it even easier, we will just put up choruses so you can just repeat the words until you learn it.

We show up each Sunday, play our updated music, see that the people responded by singing and raising their hands. We preach our well-crafted sermons and see ten people saved over the course of the year, and we think we are doing good church.

But we have it all wrong. When are we going to learn that God is attracted to broken things? You don't have to look hard in the scriptures to notice that Jesus was not spending time with

people who had it all together. Out of all the stories listed in the Bible, has it ever occurred to you that Christ was only touching the weak, sick, and feeble? Did it ever occur to you that Christ was never ministering to the rich, famous, and elite? Yet we are building our churches on the latter instead of the former.

We no longer want the messed-up people; we want the people who have it all together. Our desire is to build churches with

people who can help us fund our mission trips, support our Vacation Bible School, and ensure us that we can meet our budget that grows by 10 percent every year.

I understand that is what you want, but is that what God wants?

If God is attracted to broken people, then why are we running away from things that are broken? Why do we see a person that doesn't have it all together, but we push them onto someone else? Are we afraid we might catch their sin-sickness? Or are we just getting too close to our own sins that we have to stay away in efforts to keep our discretion hidden?

Broken people need to be healed. God's plan for this healing to take place comes through the means of confession. I don't under- stand how it all works. I can't get all scientific on you to describe the intrinsic process of what happens to you emotionally once you share your deepest secrets. All I know is this - God instructed it. I have tried it, and it works.

In our story, David had a guy by the name of Nathan. Nathan was the type of guy who was not afraid to confront the king of Israel. These two guys have a relationship where they could share and talk to each other without fear of gossip or death. Nathan called David out on his sin with Bathsheba, and it was the confession of David that led to his forgiveness and healing.

Who are you talking to? Do you have that one person that you can call up when you have messed up? We all need someone that we can rely on when life is starting to get hard. It's not a sign of weakness but a sign of maturity. Quit pretending like you have it all figured out. We know you don't. The appeal to the church is this: create an atmosphere for confessions and not just a service built around worship. David showed us in our text that worship has a role, but it takes place after he had his moment of brokenness. Don't assume that tears during a song are brokenness.

Before you start crafting your services for this next week, let's define true brokenness and then compare your service lineup with this definition. *Brokenness*: "being broken or crushed in spirit over sin."

The reason I am pushing the churches while encouraging the reader has to do with the atmosphere you create for your worshipers. A service that encourages confession will allow the people to feel more comfortable about releasing the pain and heaviness of their sin. A church that pushes for perfection that treats everyone like they already have it all together will continue to push the people to put on their mask to attend your services.

The reason many members are not getting healed from their sin-sickness is simply because we are not promoting brokenness, but rather a life that has it all together. We are not pushing confession time because we had much rather gossip.

The pastor is the leader. We are not to just lead the business meetings and the preaching schedule for the next year. The members are looking to us to give an example of what it means to live according to God's Word. When they never hear about our faults and failures, they assume the position that we are perfect. It builds a wall between the pastor and the parishioner that keeps them from confessing or sharing their mistakes.

I know in biblical times the people were forced to go and confess their sins to a priest. He would then in turn go and apply the blood on the Day of Atonement. Fast-forward to the New Testament, and we have Jesus Christ, who took care of the blood sacrifice when he died on the cross.

But are we missing out on something that these people were able to experience by having someone they can go too? I know you who are spiritual are suggesting that we have Jesus Christ, who is our High Priest sitting at the right hand of God, making those intercessions for us. Then why did God come back with "Confess your sins one to another"? (James 5:16). Was telling

Jesus not good enough, or is this accountability move a healing mechanism?

As pastors and church leaders, let's lead by example. It's okay for you to admit that you don't have it all together. We ask the church not to place us on a pedestal, but we are guilty of trying to put ourselves there and then must deal with consequences privately when we can't stay there.

The church doesn't need to know you are perfect. They need us to show them how to respond when we fail. I wish we could be the people of God that our church members think we are, but we're not, and it's okay to admit that. It's not popular, and it's not easy, but it sure is freeing!

Healing comes with confession. Confession comes after you experience a time of brokenness. Find that someone you can trust. That's when the healing begins.

CHAPTER 9
Demon Free

David therefore inquired of God for the child;
and David fasted and went and lay all night
on the ground.
                                    —2 Samuel 12:16

David was hurting. He had become attached to something that was never meant to be his. He had relations with someone who belongs to another soldier. Now the king finds himself in public humiliation for his actions. He is broken over his sin. He has placed himself on the floor in full-blown fasting and prayer. He means business right now. This situation that involved adultery and murder is not only affecting his testimony, but it is now affecting his kid.

You feel as though you can handle the pain until you start seeing it affect those you love the most. When your actions start breaking the heart of those closest to you, you will find yourself lying on the floor in full exposure to get things right.

I know all about it because . . . I am David!

I was in great pain. I didn't know what to do. Why could I not get a grip on what was taking place in my life? I remember hearing sermons on just saying no to sin, and yes to Jesus. The problem was in the fact that my desires were more powerful than my words. I wanted to be fixed. I wanted to be healed, but the biggest issue I had was having to keep it all a secret for the danger of people finding out and then exposing me.

I AM DAVID!

Mickey Bell

What would the church do?

Would they fire me, or would they help me?

Would they love me, or would they hate me?

Would they surround me and restore me, or would they poke fun at me and laugh me out of town?

The battle that was taking place within me was actually taking over me. I was reaching out to people for help, but since I wasn't being totally honest with them, they couldn't be of great help to me. You can't provide answers to unasked questions. Growing up, I had always heard of people dealing with various addictions, but no one ever talked about having a demon of sexual perversion. Was it too much for people to handle? Don't tell me I am the first one that has had to deal with this.

We heard a lot about pornography and the struggles that is causes, but no one ever dealt with the addiction of having to have it. They acted like it was just something we could turn off. Like telling a heroin addict, "Just put the pipe down."

I don't think I am the first man to have these types of issues.

I don't think I am the first pastor that has had to deal with this. So why is it that no one is talking about it? We will mention the statistics when it comes to pornography use, but no one talks about the access it gives to the inside of your heart and brain. We are bad to just preach and teach on the symptoms instead of getting to the root of the problem.

How about those who were touched before they ever watched porn? How about those who were served as a sexual playground for others before they ever reached puberty? What about those who have strongholds on their life they never asked to receive?

When it comes to the oppression of pornography, we can justify that it's not hurting anyone because it just involves us and our mind. But when you click on the website or view the e-mail, you have just opened the door and allowed a demon complete access to your life. When you submit to a text or e-mail conversation that allows someone into your inner thoughts and feelings, you have opened the gate to your emotions. The reason you are a mess now is simply because you have given too many people the key to yourself.

We justify our text messages and our Facebook messages as nothing wrong since we are not looking at pictures of nakedness. But rest assured, those comments and conversations are grabbing a hold of you and will not let go. Let me just tell you this: the enemy doesn't leave as easily as he walked in.

Can I be honest with you? It is so easy to flirt and start a conversation. One look or one comment can you have you knee-deep into a conversational relationship that causes you to desire for it to progress. It's everywhere you turn. Once you bite the apple, you start noticing apple trees all along your route of life.

When you put yourself out there and realize that you can never bring it back, you start to panic. You feel the battle raging inside of you. You are shaking from fear of being exposed. You are fearful of what might come of this. I know because I have been right where you are.

It's hard enough for any individual to come to terms with this subject matter, but my heart goes out right now to every minister or Christian in service that is reading this. No doubt you have an extra weight of concern. You are not subject to just losing your marriage or family; you have the opportunity right now to lose your life.

I AM DAVID!

Mickey Bell

I remember being on the road during the month of December.

I was broken. I was in torment. I had hurt those that I love so much. Once again, my demons had overtaken the situation and exposed me for the man I was. I had reached the point that I was done.

While sitting at a stop light, I had demons pursuing me to run away. They were ever present before me, and I was entertaining their thoughts, their slick suggestions of me ending it all. I had the choice of turning one way to go home or turn the opposite and disappear.

In my mind, by disappearing, everything would work out. If I could just leave, then Wendy and Logan could have a much better life. I mean, come on, you have heard what it has been like to be married to me. It's not been a great honeymoon, by no means. Even if Wendy ended up being alone, at least she wouldn't be hurting anymore. At least I would not be subjecting her to the torment and pain of the life I have been through.

I was tired of being the butt of jokes from other church people. I was tired of the whispers that were going on behind my back. I was tired of looking at myself in the mirror and having to deal with the comparison of what I could have been without all these issues.

The thoughts of letting people down or giving them a reason to ignore me was too much. I had decided that all church people were the same. They are okay with you as long as they get your best. The moment you show a different side that they can't handle, then they had just rather you be dead than to continue living. I didn't want to continue to live.

Within our church family, a dear couple had begun attending

our services who were different than any others that had come and gone. I can only describe them as spirit-filled prayer warriors. I don't use the word *warrior* as just any other word. This couple knew how to go to war with demons . . . and win!

I never really understood how they ended up at our church. Little did I know, they were sent there for me. In the midst of my pain, they reached out to me, and for some reason, for the first time in my life, I was able to respond. I had reached out for help that was offered before, but they were only helping the symptoms. I knew this time we were dealing with the root of the problem. I was at the point in my life that I was either going to get this out of me or it was going to kill me.

All I knew to do was to pick up the phone and call Mr. Bob and Mrs. Donna. I don't know how they were able to understand me on that call because I was already into what we call the "ugly" cry. While they may not have been able to understand the words, I was trying to say, they understood the pain and hurt that I was dealing with. They saw it as a moment to fight with a brother instead of shooting him while he was down.

Instead of judging me, they welcomed me into their home. Little did I know that I was on my way to a worship service, much like David encountered when his child was sick. It wasn't being held at an actual church, but a home where war was about to take place.

I had no idea what to expect. What was even more surprising to me was to see Wendy, my bride, sitting there with them waiting on me. All I ever wanted in my life was someone who would never leave me like so many others have done. I just wanted to know that I had someone in my life that would stay with me. It was in that moment that I finally realized why I took that girl with naturally long and curly hair out for lunch. I am not so sure we were meant for each other, but I know to this day that she was meant for me.

The moment I stepped foot in that house, I felt as though I was standing on holy ground. I saw firsthand that God had chosen someone for me that I would have never chosen for myself. He gave me someone that when she had every reason to leave, she didn't. She should have. She had every right to leave me in my pain and misery. I remember walking in the door and the prayer service starting.

I hit the floor face-first with so much power that I don't remember everything that happened next. I just know there was a lot of screaming on my part as I began to release, through my crying and pain, all that I had kept locked up inside of me.

This was not a normal prayer service. I was calling things out that had tormented me all my life. Things that I had kept hidden for so long, afraid of what others would think of me. I was calling out things that once were an embarrassment. Things that would have caused most people to run. I was not bothered by who was there who wasn't there; the main attraction for this night was the move of the Holy Spirit in my life.

When I had no words left to say, my prayer was simply the moans and groans of all the heartache and pain that had built up inside of me. I could hear that laughter of the enemy as I found myself fully exposed. I could feel the finger pointing from people who were not present, but who had made their decision about me.

I could sense the judgment of other pastors that I had looked up too. I was feeling anxiety in knowing that many of them would never want to have anything to do with me again.

But on this particular night, I didn't care. I was getting set free!

My freedom was not coming at the cost of others but at the death and resurrection of my Savior. As demons laughed at me, I just continued to pray and scream out my confessions.

Moment by moment, I could feel the release of the demons that had been tormenting me. Not only from the sexual perversion, but from the pain of comparison and entitlement. I no longer wanted to be the best, I just wanted to be me. The me that wanted to be set free. My outlook was changing. How I viewed myself was changing.

It was in that moment when I came to myself; Mrs. Donna was standing in front of me, saying with a bold voice, "I release you from the abandonment of your father." Oh, my goodness, how did she know? How could she know?

She knew only part of the testimony that I was willing to share, but how did she know this was a problem for me. I didn't have time to figure it all out. Because in that moment, the Holy Ghost of God hit me in such a way that I felt a heaviness on my heart for a split second. It happened the moment she called it forth, and when she gave the command for it to release me, words cannot describe that feeling of freedom that I felt. It let go!

I was so weak I could not stand up on my own two feet. I had forgotten where I was. As things started to clear up, I looked up, and the first person I saw sitting there was my Wendy. The one who promised to never leave me in sickness or in health. She just didn't know when she made that commitment just how sick I really was, but that didn't scare her away. God gave me someone that would stick with me in this journey to total freedom.

For the first time in the history of our relationship, I was completely exposed for her to see. If she was going to run, this would be the time to do it. This is her perfect opportunity, but instead of leaving me, she embraced me. She didn't point her finger of judgment; she put her arms of love around me.

I am sure many of you don't know how to process what I have shared with you. You don't have to tell me your beliefs when it comes to demons. There's no need for you to question my story or this experience. I was there when it happened, and I guess I ought to know.

That day, God broke the chains of bondage from abandonment that have been clamped on me at a young age. The chains of sexual perversion that had been indoctrinated into me when I was just a child. The havoc the devil has caused for me and my family for the past forty-three years. It's all been broken, and my life is forever changed. I no longer seek your approval because God set me free, and that's all that matters.

When David was confronted by his staff concerning the sick child that is now dead, the actions of the king was a bit astonishing. Even though God had taken the child that was born out of an adulterous affair, David felt the need to go and worship. What? He worshiped?

Instead of going home to mope around, he went to church. Wait, God allowed David to go through all this pain, and he was still willing to worship?

After his burden was lifted, he could only think of one place he wanted to be, and that was in the presence of his heavenly Father.

I hear the whispers behind my back. I see the heads turning, so people don't have to make eye contact with me in public. I sense the judgment of people on why I continue to pastor Grace Church Bessemer. For many, I am not qualified. By many standards in today's churches, I am unfit to be a pastor. As though   all   the   other

pastors are living perfect lives. Just because my sins and shortcomings may be something you never will have to deal with doesn't make my indiscretion more severe than yours.

That is beside the point. Take a person addicted to drugs for twenty years and let him get delivered, and we will pay large offerings to bring them in to share their testimony to scare our teens. Let a pastor share his deliverance story, and he gets run out of town.

I get it. I understand the fact that I may never pastor another church outside Grace Church Bessemer. Many congregations would never call me to pastor, much less preach in their pulpits ever again because I am too nasty. That's okay. I am settled within the calling that is on my life.

God has shown me a vision. I have received sight of the future when other men, like me, come to grips with their own demons. They currently have nowhere to run. Our churches are too clean. Our pastors don't want to get dirty. They simply want to continue to pastor their routine from one year to the next without offering any hope of change. They want everything within their churches to be pristine and shiny.

Having people with real issues might mess up the flow of the offering. To help real people with real issues will cause the movement of change to first start with the pastor. So, they are afraid to mess up what they call a good "church" thing.

Others are just simply afraid of what might happen if they release the Holy Spirit within their churches. They have preached with him on a leash, and they are unsure of what might take place. The outcome could be something they can no longer control or explain.

Not me! I want to see people set free. I want you to feel what I

feel inside of me right now. There are no words that I can use to describe to you how it feels to be able to breathe without guilt. To be able to look at my wife and know that I am fully exposed.

To be able to look down at my new wedding ring that I got after my deliverance service and know that it is once again pure.

Don't get me wrong. I have my days of embarrassment, and I judge myself pretty harsh. The enemy is ever present before me to try to remind me of my past. Since he lost control of me, he has made it his goal to destroy me. He comes after my thoughts, and he uses other people to bring me down.

Well, I have made some goals for myself. I want to be able to help more people than I hurt. I am now on an all-out vengeance to take back our men. I am taking back the pastors and preachers of our churches. The enemy is no longer going to hold this over your head. He is no longer going to convince you that you are done.

Listen to me, man of God.

Listen to me, woman of God.

It's time to get clean. You can do this!

There is no reason why you should live the rest of your life under the burden of the decisions you have made. For some of you, you are heading down a very dangerous path, and this book has been placed in your hands as a warning. It's not too late to turn back, but it's time to make the turn.

When God knew you in your mother's womb, He set you apart for a purpose. Since He is an all-knowing God, He knew the end from the beginning. Which means, He called and ordained you despite you. So, God allowed you to be ordained as a minister even though He knew you had issues.

Did you hear that? In spite of your last bad decision, God still called you. In spite of knowing the mistakes you would make; He still saw a greater potential inside of you that He could use. God's decision about you doesn't always mirror the church's decision about you. He is much more loving and forgiving. Don't allow a congregation or a group of people keep you from being set free. If you lose all your friends while losing the demons who have control of you, it will still be worth it.

It seems I have been hard on the term *church*. I may have gone overboard in putting everyone in the same category. It wasn't my intention to down the church, but when things happen like I have experienced, we all feel the pain that comes more from a body of believers than those who are out in sin.

I sense our ministry in the city of Bessemer becoming more of a redemption house for those who have fallen victim to their own demons. A place where you can come for healing and deliverance. A safe place of sorts for those in high positions. A place that will not judge you, but a place that will love you to total freedom.

God told me to shine my light bright, but I didn't want too. Why would I want to display my mistakes for the entire world to see? Why would I want to give my haters more ammunition to use against me? What about those people who know parts of my story but until now didn't know all of it? What will people say?

Why would I want to go through all this again?

I will tell you why. When God set me free, He gave me a mission to get others free. That is why you receive the blessings from God. Not to stockpile for yourself, but to be able to bless others. God showed me pastors who would be calling me for help.

He showed me staff members who would come to me because they would not be able to go to their own pastors in fear of losing their jobs. He showed me business owners who are fearful of losing everything they have. He showed me government leaders who feel as though they can't come clean.

People who would run to get freedom because they finally found a place where they could open up and not feel the pressure of it being used against them. We are not here to judge or to kick you while you are down. This ministry is here to lift you up and show you a life of freedom. "So, if the Son makes you free, you will be free indeed" (John 8:36).

Alcohol-free.

Drug-free.

Sexual-perversion-free.

Demon-free!

Chapter 10
He Didn't Throw the Clay Away

Empty and broken, I came back to Him
A vessel unworthy, so scarred with
sin.
But He did not despair . . . He started over
again and I bless the day, He didn't
throw the clay away.

Those words from a gospel song have come to mean more to me now than ever before. Even though I grew up listening to this song, it wasn't until I got to this point in my life that the words actually started ministering to my situation.

In Jeremiah 18, we have a beautiful illustration of the love that our heavenly Father has for us. The picture is that of a potter who is creating something beautiful out of clay. Not just any clay, verse 4 says the potter is using clay that has been marred. When I looked up the word *marred*, I found these words to be used to describe the clay the potter was talking about: "Flaw, injure; blot. *Mar, deface, disfigure, deform* agree in applying to some form of injury."

Wow! Those words actually describe my life. I have never more felt like the clay in this story than what I feel at this moment. My life has forever been flawed. My testimony is suffering from injury. People are constantly judging my every move and treating me like I have a disease that is not only contagious, but incurable.

I have spent many days suffering from the opinions of others.

Allowing my thoughts to overtake me into thinking the worst for every situation. It's a rotten feeling to feel as though everyone has given up on you even while you are trying to bounce back. I quickly learned that everyone has a line for you. They are okay with you getting well and being set free from the demons that torment you as long as you do it before you cross the line, they have set for you.

Once you cross that line, it's as though as you are flawed goods. You are no longer usable by God. You are nothing more than scraps of clay that have been left on the floor. That was how I was living my life until I found Jeremiah 18. That's the moment I realized that they were partially right, but they were also very wrong.

They were correct in their assessment of me being a scrap of clay. A portion of a project that went wrong. A piece of scrap that many pastors and churches have thrown to the floor, never to be seen or heard from again.

But they were dead wrong when they tried to use their theology and personal opinion in an attempt to convince me that everyone viewed me that way, including the potter. But Jeremiah 18 paints a totally different picture for me, and for all of you who have found yourself pushed off the table into the floor. For those of you who feel like scraps or simply pieces of a project that can't be used again, I have good news for you. The potter of this project doesn't attend the churches that have discounted and scrapped you. He doesn't fully understand the comments that are being made about you by those who claim to be living with His love running through their veins.

Oh no! This potter sees something unique about you. Our God is

all-knowing in that he can see something about you when others just see scraps. Our God is all-powerful in that He can take literal scraps from your life and create you into something worth

displaying again. That's what I love about my heavenly Father. He is the type of potter that doesn't give up on the clay. He doesn't throw away the scraps, but He picks up the pieces and does as the song says:

> Over and over, He molds me and makes me,
> Into His likeness, He fashions the clay.
> A vessel of honor, I am today,
> All because Jesus didn't throw the clay away.

Now understand that the potter can't always be gentle when it comes to working with tough clay. He has to pound and beat it into submission, especially when the clay has been sitting in one place for too long. The potter must beat and crush the clay to cause it to reform into an element that will allow him to form what he sees in his mind.

All you see right now are scraps. All that people around you see are leftover pieces of what could have been a great life, but the potter sees something totally different. It's that difference that causes the pain of being molded into something you thought you would never be.

It's not a pleasant experience when the potter must slam the clay on the table to break it apart, but it's necessary for the creation of his vision, and then the cutting begins. The potter will take out a sharp knife, and while the clay is sitting on the potter's wheel, the blade will begin to shave off the elements of the project that are not supposed to be there.

The cutting allows the designer of our life to remove the excess that will take away the value of the final piece. So, cutting is required. That's why God has to cut us sometimes to remove the

things we have attached ourselves to. Many relationships have been cut. Many friendships had to end once the potter put the clay on the wheel. It's not that they are bad people; they are just bad for you.

We must trust the potter to know what He is doing, and just because we can't see what He sees, we still must submit to His cutting with the trust that He knows what is best. Once you have been on the bottom rung of life, it really doesn't bother you that the cutting is taking place. You are just glad someone is showing you some attention, even if it is painful.

My cutting away consisted of things I had placed on me from a very young age. The cutting was very painful and very public, but I am able to see why it had to take place. The image that I had for myself was not what the potter had in mind. I wanted to be a valuable plate to be set up and admired when the potter wanted me to be a mug that was used to refresh the user.

The lesson I am learning is that as a scrap of clay, I don't have a say into what the potter wants me to be. I simply must submit to Him, knowing that He is wanting to make me beautiful again. I say "again" because of the wording used in Jeremiah 18.

In verse 4, the text reads, "He made of clay was marred in the hand of the potter; so, he made it again into another vessel, as it seemed good to the potter to make."

First, notice that the potter chose clay that was marred. He didn't go out seeking brand-new material for this particular project. He picked up the pieces, knowing what he was working with. The verse goes on to say that he made it again.

Now I have to stop there because I was a piece of pottery that had been broken into pieces. I was the scraps of clay that once had life together, and while I saw my life on the floor, feeling rejected and unusable, the potter chose to take the pieces of my life and make "another vessel." That goes against what many churches preach and teach. They want you to believe that God will reject you and you are no longer qualified to serve. While they put limitations on people with their own judgments, God's Word plainly paints the picture of the potter creating *again* what was once broken and left on the floor.

I can't help but think of how many vessels have been left on the floor by ministries that could have done some good. How many pastors have been kicked to the wayside with the letter *A* on their chest, and told they are no longer qualified? How many singers and musicians have been kicked off the table because they didn't measure up to what the Christian society thought they should be?

It's in this moment my mind carries me back into God's Word to try to find the perfect vessels that Jesus took time with. I can't find them. I see Him picking out the messed-up, the rejected, and the sick.

He simply calls them near for a touch. I also notice that the church people were constantly walking past the sick and afflicted. They were in a hurry to get to church and didn't have time to be the church, and had it not been for Jesus noticing the broken, we would have no stories of healing and restoration in God's Word. Ah, that's a good word—*restoration*!

That's what the potter is doing when He picks up the pieces of your life and starts creating a new vessel. He is restoring what has been broken into something that can be used again. That is what I feel is my new mission in this life. To simply help fallen soldiers in God's army in their attempt to get back up again. I will not be a pastor/preacher that tells a person they are done. That is not Bible. I will not be a part of a church that cast more people out than they bring in. That is not a part of God's plan. If you reject a leader because of their dents and scratches, then what are you telling your congregation who shows up broken to pieces?

There's one more part of that text that I have to mention before I can go on. Notice the very end of that verse that says, "He made of clay was marred in the hand of the potter; so, he made it again into another vessel, as it seemed good to the potter to make."

It seemed good to the potter to make a new vessel again. I needed to hear that, so I bet you needed to hear it as well. It's not a chore for the potter to have to rebuild something. It's not a stress or a discomfort on His part to start over. God sees you as something good to rebuild. He sees the pieces of your life scattered across the floor, but He knows if He can gather up those pieces and get you back on the wheel, He can create something of value that He would be proud to put His name on.

He desires to see you succeed. He desires to see you make a comeback. He desires to see what can come of the pieces that have been left on the floor by so many other Christians. He simply needs you to make yourself available for the remolding.

Allow Him to beat the clay into submission for the reformation of your ministry. Allow the knife to cut away the parts that are not going to be a part of the new vessel. Allow the potter to mold you on the spinning wheel even when it feels you are spinning out of control. The end result is going to be amazing. There will be a time when God will remold you into a new vessel and watch the faces of your haters when He presents you again. When He takes what they have rejected, and He places you on the shelf of his most prized possessions. When He puts you back into ministry opportunities with a new outlook, a new conviction, and a new passion. You might have started out in your first ministry with the goal of building big churches. Your new goal may simply be to sweep off the pieces of broken ministries to place back on the wheel so the potter can get to work.

As a new pastor in my early thirties, I desired to be like the fine china you see that has an expensive price tag. That most sought-after design that people must have, but after going through my experience, I have come to learn that the fine china is always placed in hiding until company comes over. It's the dishes that are only brought out two maybe three times per year if any. All the other times, these dishes are simply stored and kept back out of the way.

So one has to decide if they want to be used by God as an every-day tool that will affect the lives of people, or do you simply desire to be kept so clean and out of the way that you are only noticed on special occasions?

I desire to be clean and polished so that others will accept me. I just never want to get to the place that I discount someone's use simply because they have a little dirt or scratch. People may admire the fine china that is passed down from generation to generation, but it's the coffee mug that they can't leave home without. It may get dented, and it may get scratched, but its use is desired and needed daily.

In my first ministry, I was working to impress people. People who were quick to throw me out. In my second ministry, I am working to please the potter because He saw me as good to remake. I can admit this simply because—you guessed it, ...I AM DAVID!

I AM DAVID!   Mickey Bell

David started out great and was getting so much attention to the things he was able to accomplish. I mean killing a giant and get- ting all the rewards that came with that win, but then to get all the accolades and the reputation that was noised throughout his country. He was the modern-day hero. Everyone knew his name. Little boys would pretend to be him when they were outside playing with the slingshot they asked for Christmas.

David would even become king and have the entire nation bowing at his command when at one bad moment in his life he falls off the potter's wheel. In a matter of minutes, David, the hero, was now nothing but pieces of scratched, dented clay lying on the floor, begging God to save his son.

It was in that moment of invitation David had to decide to either get back up on the potter's wheel or remain destroyed. I am glad he chose the latter. He chose to not allow his mistake to be the way he went out of this world.

And still today, people refer to him, not as the adulterer David but the psalmist David. You never heard pastors quote Psalm 23 from the cheater and murder; it's always alluded to the shepherd boy who was after God's heart. They may be talking about your mistakes now, but soon they will be talking about the masterpiece you have become. We just have to know who the potter is that is molding and remaking us. God is not basing our worth on what others may say or do. He is not concerned with their approval rating, nor should we.

We must stay in the process of becoming who God wants us to be. Remember, He doesn't throw away the pieces. He picks them up and figures out a way to use them again. I may be viewed as flawed and dented without any purpose. Don't give up on me yet. The potter still has me on the wheel, molding me into what He wants me to be. Trust me, when He is finished with

Mickey Bell

me, I will be amazing.

Chapter 11
Do I Get Another Chance?

"A church is a hospital for sinners, not a museum for saints." Throughout this book, I have made some pretty strong statements about the church and how they are not as forgiving as others would expect them to be. Let me say this clearly—not all churches are that way. There are some great places of worship led by great leaders who have a heart for the brokenhearted.

Please don't take my viewpoint that all churches are bad except the one I pastor because that is certainly not the case, but if you are reading this after being hurt by a church, then I want you to know that it's common, but they are not all that way.

I just find it hard to believe that we claim to live by God's Word, yet we want to input our own thoughts and judgments in place of where God puts his. He says forgive seventy times seven, and many of us can't even make it to the seven.

In the last chapter, my goal was to show you an illustration from God's Word just how he feels about sinners. We know he loves them because He sent His one-of-a-kind Son to die for us. I have

noticed that once people get into a position of authority within the local church, they assume the responsibility of the Holy Spirit. They find themselves serving in the capacity of the holiness police, and once you have been found guilty, then you are done. But I just can't find that in the scriptures.

Take for instance Ezekiel 37. Just in case you are not familiar with the text, let me give it to you: "The hand of the Lord came upon me and brought me out in the Spirit of the Lord, and set me down in the midst of the valley; and it *was* full of bones."

The prophet was taken to a place that many of us just as soon stay away from. This is not a place where you want to vacation or spend your holidays, yet many will. The Bible describes it as "the middle of the valley."

While we all have valley moments in our life, and while they serve as a location for learning, this was never a place for you to camp out. This was strictly a place in between two mountains where you could be schooled, or examined, while making your way to your next high moment in life. But for some reason, we feel the need to hang out there longer than what was ever intended.

I want you to know that this is not a fun place to be. You don't come here expecting things to be great. In fact, you throw one party while you are there, and it's a pity party. You get mad if no one wants to come down into your valley to celebrate with you.

It's not a safe place to be either. Many bad decisions have been made, and many life-altering decisions have been made in this location. Never ever make any decisions when you find yourself camping out in the valley. Here your vision is not clear. You will end up deciding on key factors of your life while you are in a dry place.

When you find yourself in a valley, the only thing that should concern you should be how to get out, not finding another spouse or a better job. There is something about being in the

valley that causes you to become delusional. You can't think straight, and you end up making the wrong decisions.

130

If you find yourself sitting in a valley while reading this book, listen to me. This valley was never meant to become your destination. It was simply a part of the route that you are taking. You might have ended up here because of a mistake. A bad decision might have caused your GPS to take you through this particular location. No matter what got you here, you are not supposed to stay here.

Keep walking! Don't stop moving and decide that this is your new address. No! This is just a small moment in time.

The prophet Ezekiel found himself looking at a valley full of dry bones. Bones that belonged to people just like you who found themselves walking through this valley, but for some reason decided to stop moving. For some reason, they arrived at a moment in their life where they thought this valley was their destination. They arrived in a valley and had no one to encourage them to keep moving. They decided that this was it, and they had no other reason to keep living.

So now this prophet is looking at a pile of bones who simply gave up and quit. Don't let this be you. Don't you dare buy into the lie from the pits of hell that this is your end. This is just a sidetrack of the main path of your journey. Learn what you are supposed to learn while in this valley, but don't you dare stay here. This valley was built for learning, not for living.

As Ezekiel peered across the valley to a pile of bones, I can't help but wonder what he was thinking. I know what I would be thinking because I am thinking it now. I wonder if any of these bones belonged to the person that had the cure for cancer, but because he gave up too quickly, now many others must suffer.

I can't help but think that maybe within these piles of bones, there was an individual who had the cure for mental illness or the answer to all these mass shootings. Was there a body within these bones that had the answer for racism? Did one of those bodies have the mind to stop miscarriages?

Now all of a sudden, these bones mean something to us. We are not just looking at a pile of people we can just forget about. These people who quit living and quit dreaming could have made a major impact in our lives today, but we will never know simply because they quit.

Don't you dare quit. There is something inside of you that this world needs. You have the message that is going to save thousands. You have the thoughts that will create job opportunities. You have the answer to many of life's questions that people need to hear. Don't you dare give up on me. I am not going to allow you to become these bones. I am not going to allow you to stop living and stop dreaming just because you have found yourself in the middle of a valley.

> Then He caused me to pass by them all around, and behold, *there were* very many in the open valley; and indeed, *they were* very dry. The text goes out of its way to describe these bones as "very dry," meaning they have been here for a while. I wonder how many of these bones were dropped off here because churches gave up on them? Could any of these bones be former deacons or elders who had an affair, and the church deported them to this valley instead of restoring them to service?

I don't know how long it takes for bones to become dry, but these bones have been in the valley too long because when the prophet saw them, he saw very dry bones.

> And He said to me, "Son of man, can these
> bones live?" So, I answered, "O Lord God, you
> know."

The Lord asked the prophet a question that is very important. God knows they can live, but He needs to see if this preacher believes it. He needs to make sure he has the correct pastor standing over these bones. God doesn't need a prophet who sees these bones as they are currently. He needs to make sure He has a man of God who sees what these bones can become.

We think anyone can just be a pastor. They may be good at hospital visits, and they may have finished a seminary degree, but if you are unable to look at dry bones and see potential, then you are not the prophet for this job. Ezekiel has to prove that he believes that there is life still in these bones even though they are lifeless in the middle of a valley.

How can the bones that sit in our congregations every week feel like they can have a better life if the person standing before them doesn't believe it? That's why I am so glad you have this book in your hands. While you may not have a person speaking over you, allow me to speak over you.

> Again, He said to me, "Prophesy to these
> bones, and say to them, 'O dry bones, hear
> the word of the Lord!'"

After God checked the belief system of the prophet, He instructed him to prophesy over these bones. He didn't say *speak*, He said *prophesy*. If I speak to the bones, I will only describe what I see in their current condition. If I only speak to the problem, then I will continuously beat them up with my words in yelling at them from God's Word on what caused this condition.

Listen, pastor, they know what sent them to the valley. They know the sin that caused them to lose it all. They don't need someone telling them how they got there, they need someone to tell them how to get out. We send more people to hell in telling them what not to do because of sin than telling them what they need to do to get out of sin.

The Lord said to prophesy, not gossip. He didn't tell this pastor to go to the preacher's meeting on Monday and share with the other "godly" men what he saw. He didn't say pick up the phone and call the other churches in your area and tell them everything you know. He said, "Prophesy to these bones."

I know what everyone else is saying. I know the unbelief that is being sown through the mouths of so many others, but, prophet, tell these bones to live. Tell these bones to get up and dust themselves off. Tell these bones they still have a future.

That is the whole purpose of me writing this book. I may not be able to get you to our church. I may not ever meet you face-to- face in service where you hear me preach a message. So, if you don't mind, let me use this time to prophesy over the "very dry bones" that I see holding this book.

You are not destined for defeat, but rather you have already won. Don't allow the enemy to convince you that you are done. Don't allow the demons of hell to use other church members and leaders to keep you down. I speak life over these bones. I call forth every bone to fall back into place. I call forth the muscle that is needed to move these bones. I pray strength over your life. Get up, man of God. Get up, woman of God. You were never intended to stay here.

I AM DAVID!

In Psalm 23, the psalmist David didn't say, "Yeah, though I camp out in the valley of the shadow of death." No! He said, "Yeah though I *walk through* the valley of the shadow of death." You were never supposed to stop walking.

Get up and find your walking shoes. Lace up your running shoes because it is time to get out of this valley and get back to doing what God has called you to do. Wipe off the dust of rejection. Wash off the nastiness of religious judgment.

You have a job to do. There's a ministry with your name on it. Watch this closely. The Lord asked the prophet this very important question: "Can these bones live *again*?" See, our heavenly Father is not a one-and-done type of God. He is giving these bones another chance to live. He is calling them forth to serve again, and that is what I am doing for you.

I am calling you to live again. Love again. Serve again. Preach again. Minister again. I am calling these bones to come together and do what others said could never be done.

Chapter 12
Ministry Suicide

So why share this with you, whom I know and many I do not know? Because just like me, you are bound, and the longer you wait about breaking free, the worse it will get. I am no longer on a mission to pastor a big church. I am on the mission to help get people free.

Even for David, he was unable to build the temple that he had as a goal from an early age as king, but that didn't stop him from getting all the materials together so his son could build the house of God.

I get it, this is ministry suicide. I know I have lost a lot of respect from a lot of people by sharing all this with you. Some may not ever look at me the same, but that's okay. My freedom wasn't for them, it was for me and for you.

My family is still together only by the grace of God. I will continue to serve at Grace Church Bessemer as long as messed-up people continue to come, knowing firsthand that their pastor has been messed up himself.

So how do we wrap this up? After all David did that was wrong, after all David did that was correct, in Acts 13:22, God said this about David: "I have found David, son of Jesse, a man after my own heart."

For the rest of my days, I will serve the Lord that not only saved me at eight years old, but also the God that set me free at age forty-three. My goal is to be able to have God say the same thing about me.

There are people who will continue to hate me. There will be people who will continue to despise me. You may even become a person who rejects me. But I am not here to please people anymore, and I am not afraid of people leaving me because that demon has been cast away from me, plus God said he would never leave me nor forsake me. To boot, I still have Wendy and Logan.

Together, we will continue to live our life serving God, and hopefully one day, I will hear him say, "I have found Mickey, son of Ed Bell, a man after my own heart."

Because . . . I AM DAVID.

Bonus Material

If you read the forward at the beginning of the book, then you met Dr. Barry Cosper. This man literally saved my life, my marriage, and my ministry. In talking with him about this book, he started sharing with me how many churches run from the calling of church discipline simply because they are not fully aware of the process. With his permission, I wanted to include an excerpt from his book, "*A Matter of the Heart – A Ministry of Restoration*" to give you an idea as to how you should look at church discipline and the ministry of restoration.

The decline of church discipline has left a visible mark upon the contemporary church. Dr. Al Mohler, president of the Southern Baptist Theological Seminary in Louisville, Kentucky, described the decline of church discipline as the "most visible failure of the contemporary church."[1] He went on to describe the contemporary church as one that "sees itself as a voluntary association of autonomous members with minimal moral accountability to God, much less to each other."[2]

Church discipline, in its biblical context, is an act of love. Church discipline is not a church board acting as a police department. Church discipline is a ministry of love and discipleship by the people of God to assist fellow Christians who fall into sin. Matthew 18 contains the biblical foundation and characteristics that are necessary ingredients for an active discipline ministry. The components include simple humility (18:1-6), frank honesty (18:15-17), united prayer (18:19-20), and a forgiving spirit (18:21-35).[3] In church discipline, the entire church only gets involved if the individuals cannot reconcile conflict or open sin.

For church discipline to work effectively, the church must have a healthy spiritual atmosphere. Church discipline is not a vindictive act or an act of hatred. Instead, church discipline is an act of love and concern in that the purpose throughout the process is restoration. As restoration takes place, the objective is to restore the individual to the point of usefulness again in service to Jesus Christ. Church discipline involves rescuing the individual from a continual lifestyle of sin.

The discipline described in 1 Corinthians 5 contained three objectives. The discipline is intended "for the good of the offender (5:1-5), for the good of the congregation (5:6-8), and for the good of the unsaved society (5:9-13)."[4] Even with the objections in mind, some church members perceive church discipline as problematic and troublesome. These perceptions are influenced by abuse from the past that resulted in scars and regrets instead of celebrations occurring from re-claiming the fallen Christian and total restoration. The dismal results of the history, as regrettable as it could be, should not cause a church to dispense with church discipline. The desires to reclaim and restore a fallen Christian should outweigh any negatives that could prohibit the practice of church discipline in a church.

The joy of restoration is an empowering spiritual experience that enables a church to rise above the cruel traditions of the past and experience the positive values of church discipline. As church discipline is conducted lovingly with the intent of restoring the church family is united. Christ is honored. A secular world that is not impressed by churches that tolerate open sin will take notice of changed and transformed lives that resulted from a redemptive ministry called church discipline by churches who dared to care.

As church discipline is an integral part of the Christian life, so is church discipline an essential part of the life of the church. The church is to reflect the spirit of Christ and be "a bastion of purity in the midst of a crooked generation."[5]

> The church's goal is not primarily to become a
> particular interest group crusading against
> abortionists, homosexuals, and other sinners
> – but to be examples of upright living amid
> the darkness all around us. The church is to
> deal with any hint of sexual, social, or
> economic scandal within its ranks (1
> Corinthians 5:9-13). We are to bring ourselves
> under the rule of Christ and to lead as many
> people as possible to the One who can change
> human hearts.[6]

The subject of church discipline provokes varied and, at times, intense reactions. Bad experiences and horror stories of abused practices that were characterized as heavy-handed or unwise have caused many Christians to view church discipline with disdain. However, the absence of church discipline is more damaging to both Christians and churches. Church discipline has been defined as "an expression of Christian love and an important aspect of making disciples."[7]

Another defined church discipline as "God's loving plan for restoring sinning saints."[8] J. Carl Laney further emphasizes that restoration is the purpose of church discipline and not ruination.[9]

Church discipline has been described as a result of evangelism. Through evangelism "the church ministers to those outside the church who are in bondage to sin while congregational discipline ministers to those within the church who are in bondage to sin."[10] Church discipline may also be defined as "the confrontive and corrective measures taken by individuals, church leaders, or the congregation regarding a matter of sin in the life of a believer."[11] From a biblical standpoint, church discipline is designed to awaken people to the tragedy of sin in a Christian's life and move him or her to repentance. Even though restoration is the primary purpose of church discipline, sometimes church discipline fails. The failure can be attributed to gossip about the fallen Christian's sin traveling through the church grapevine at rapid speed. The result is an embarrassment for the fallen Christian as he or she leaves the church never to return.

What is church discipline? Church discipline is a necessary component of the church. Church discipline is vital to the church to retain the purity, power, and progress of the church. The basis for church discipline is the divine authority of the Bible. Therefore, the church has a responsibility to implement church discipline both as a formative or preventive and corrective or excessive practice. Formative discipline involves the teaching and training of believers, so they become mature disciples. Corrective discipline is used when a believer refuses to be disciplined by the Bible in a formative manner. Therefore, church discipline may be broadly defined as the "confrontive and corrective means taken by an individual, church leaders, or the congregation regarding a matter of sin."

The pattern for the basis of church discipline is multi-faceted. First, church discipline is patterned from the biblical teaching that the Lord himself disciplines His children (Hebrews 12:6). Furthermore, the Lord delegates to the church the discipline of the church family (1 Corinthians 5:12-13; 2 Corinthians 2:6).

Second, church discipline emphasizes the holy character of God (1 Peter 1:16: Hebrews 12:11). As God's character is holy, so is the church to be holy. The church is to remove the leaven from the ranks (1 Corinthians 5:6-8). The failure to deal with unrepentant sin reveals a compromised state that brings irreparable harm to the name of God.

Third, church discipline is based on the commands of Scripture.

Scripture gives God's directives and directions on how to implement an effective ministry of church discipline. Failure to implement and practice church discipline reveals and demonstrates a lack of belief in the authority of the Bible (1 Corinthians 5:1-13; Matthew 18:17-18; Titus 3:10; 2 Thessalonians 3:6-15; 1 Timothy 5:20; Galatians 6:1).

As the pattern of church discipline is established, the purposes of church discipline are set forth to reveal how a church can remain spiritually healthy. A church obedient to the divine authority of Scripture will follow the following biblical purposes.

> 1. Church discipline is to bring glory to God and to enhance the testimony of the flock.

> 2. Church discipline is to restore, heal, and build up sinning believers (Matthew 18:15; 2 Thessalonians 2:14-15; Hebrews 12:10-13; Galatians 6:1-2; James 5:20).

> 3. Church discipline is to produce a healthy faith, one sound in doctrine (Titus 1:13; 1 Timothy 1:19-20).

> 4. Church discipline is to silence false teachers and their influence in the church (Titus 1:10-11).

> 5. Church discipline is to set an example for the rest of the body and promote Godly fear (1 Timothy 5:20).

6. Church discipline is to protect the church against the destructive consequences that occur when churches fail to carry out church discipline.[14]

The disregard of church discipline within the church produces four adverse situations that cannot be easily ignored. The four adverse conditions are the loss of purity, power, progress, and purpose.[15]

The church becomes subject to moral decay and impure doctrinal influences with the loss of purity. The church is to remove the leaven from its midst (1 Corinthians 5:6-7) or have the church affected negatively. The Corinthian church showed a lack of concern for purity and paid the price. Their lack of discipline for the moral issue of incest created suffering within the church. The suffering created a negative spiral that produced "lawsuits, misused their liberty, profaned the Lord's Supper, neglected the primacy of love, failed to regulate the use of their gifts, and questioned the resurrection."[16]

The unrepented and blatant practice of sin grieves the Holy Spirit and quenches the power of the Holy Spirit (1 Thessalonians 5:19). Not only does the church lose its power, but it also becomes subject to its carnal practices. The church loses its power as the Holy Spirit abandons the church due to the unrepented sin problem. The only solution is for the church to deal with the sin problem, so the blessing of the Lord may return. This principle is illustrated in Joshua 7 with the sin of Achan.

The loss of progress is also a result of a church that does not practice church discipline. The loss of progress is noted through the decline of the church. The church may want to grow, may want to reach people for Christ, and want to be a positive influence in the community, but a church that is indifferent to its sin problem will not have the respect of the local community. Regardless of the current promotional campaign measures that are put in place for damage control, the church will not reach its desired objectives. Revelation 2:5 provides an instructive principle for a church in decline due to sin. A church is to

remember, repent, and return to its first love.

A church that does not practice church discipline will lose its purpose. Various polls reveal that the modern church is perceived as being no different than the secular world.

Furthermore, people spend their everyday lives attempting to survive what is recognized as a rat race, denying authenticity and personal fulfillment. God has a plan for the church. It is to be holy and be entirely different from the world while proclaiming the excellencies of God in Christ (1 Timothy 1:14-16; 2:9-15). A church that lives up to the calling of God will have a positive impact upon the attitudes, values, morals, and lifestyles of people looking for sensible answers to the perplexing problems experienced in daily living.

The practice of church discipline has many modern-day objectors. The objections can be attributed to "instances when people have been unceremoniously 'booted' out of a church by a pulpit despot, a high-handed church clique, or perhaps even a whole church, yet one who was ignorant and unspiritual."[17] Unfortunately, innocent people that had no real blame according to the biblical teaching or in the Lord's sight have been unjustly treated. The fear of repeated unjust practices has created a backlash of objections to the modern practice of church discipline. However, when church discipline is researched

A recommendation to the practice of church discipline is "don't do it."[18] Do not become involved in church discipline until you follow Jesus' instruction in Luke 14:25-33. This recommendation is not a recommendation for delayed obedience. Instead, it is a recommendation to count the cost of such a ministry of restoration. It is also a recommendation that the church is spiritually prepared for such an endeavor of reclaiming fallen Christians.

To prepare the church spiritually, the church must be taught, trained, and equipped with the following five principles.[19] First, the church is to be encouraged to practice humility. Through the practice of humility, people will have the opportunity to see if they were mistaken regarding their spiritual states. The church is to examine itself to see if it is also in the faith.

Second, the church is to be taught the biblical understanding of church membership. Many do not understand discipline due to their lack of understanding of membership. Membership is a congregational relationship that rises above individual acts. An individual's membership is based on congregational approval. Membership is not automatically voided due to a member leaving as a result of unrepentant sin. The church is to notify a church of the unrepentant sinner's condition and the reason for leaving.

Jonathan Leeman describes the leaving of a church due to unrepentant sin as a "preemptive resignation – a get out of jail free card."[20] From a civil point of view, the argument could insist in a democratic civil society that the church should be classified as a "voluntary organization."

Third, the pastor is to pray that God will help him to model biblical church discipline to Christians in the church. The modeling will take place through the public teaching of the biblical text regarding church discipline. Further modeling will take place as he ministers to families and individuals. As he works to create an atmosphere of discipleship, he will assist Christians in their understanding that an essential part of following Christ is to assist others in following Christ through evangelism and discipleship. Through the modeling, Christians will learn that "the Christian life is personal, but not private."[23]

Fourth, the pastor is to prepare the church's written constitution and by-laws. The constitution and by-laws will deal with legal matters as well as church membership requirements. These principles will be taught to the whole church and utilized in new member classes. Both membership and discipline are a part of the teaching process.

Fifth, as pastor and spiritual leader in pulpit ministry, keep the teaching and preaching of what is a Christian as a top priority. The church is taught that the church is composed of sinners who have repented of their sin and trusted Christ alone as their Savior and Lord. As the spiritual leader, the gospel will be the foundation for teaching and developing the church. The spiritual leader will lead the church to adopt church discipline as a part of discipleship ministry.

The spiritual leader who uses the five principles will find his church in a state of spiritual readiness and preparedness to practice church discipline as a redemptive and compassionate act of restoration. The church will be ready to exercise church discipline when the following characterizations are manifested.

- The leaders understand it, agree with it, and perceive its importance (mature leadership shared among several elders is consistent with Scripture and very helpful or leading a church through potentially volatile discussions).

- The congregation is united in understanding that such discipline is biblical.

- The membership consists mainly of people who regularly hear your sermons.

• A particularly clear case comes along in which your members would reasonably and unitedly perceive that excommunication could occur if the fallen Christian refuses and rejects restoration.[24]

One hundred fifty years ago, John Dagg stated that "when discipline leaves a church, Christ goes with it."[25] During that time, Baptists and other evangelicals practiced church discipline extensively. In the last fifty years, the practice of church discipline has been abandoned by evangelicals. Churches in the West have neglected church discipline for three generations.

Church discipline is vital to the spiritual health of any church.

Instead of rejecting church discipline from past horror stories or as outdated and irrelevant, may the church discover it as a "loving, provocative, attractive, distinct, respectful, gracious act of obedience and mercy, and that it helps to build a church that brings glory to God."[26]

About the Author

Mickey Bell is a pastor, musician, radio show host, and entertainer. His work has won him many awards as a producer and radio show host. As a musician, he has already been inducted into the Gospel Music Hall of Fame (GMA) 2017. He is the founding and senior pastor of Grace Church Bessemer in the state of Alabama.

He and his wife, Wendy, have one daughter named Brindley Logan. They are three very dedicated workers to the cause of Christ all across America and around the world.

BIBLIOGRAPHY

[1] Al Mohler, Jr., "Church Discipline: The Missing Mark," Web page; available from http://www.the-highway.com/discipline-Mohlr.html; Internet; accessed 16 September 2009.

[2] Ibid.

[3] Harold S. Martin, "Biblical Study of Church Discipline," Brethren Revival Fellowship, Editorial July/August 1993, Volume 28, Number 4, Web page; available from http://www.brfwitness.org/?p=611& print=1; Internet; accessed 16 September 2009.

[4] Ibid.

[5] Ibid.

[6] Ibid.

[7] Stuart Murray, Explaining Church Discipline (Tonbridge, Kent, England: Sovereign World Limited, 1995), 5.

[8] J. Carl Laney, A Guide to Church Discipline (Minneapolis, MN: Bethany House Publishers, 1985), 14.

[9] Ibid.

[10] Ibid.

[11] Ibid.

[12] Ibid., 14.

[13] Ibid.

[14] J. Hampton Keathley, III, "Church Discipline," published on Bible.org, May 2004, Web page; available from http://bible.org/print/532;Internet; accessed 2 August 2011.

[15] Ibid.

[16] Laney, 20.

[17] Mohler, Jr., op. Cit.

[18] Mark Dever, "'Don't do it' Why you Shouldn't Practice Church Discipline." Web page; available from http://www.9marks.org/CC/CDA?Content_ Blocks? CC_Printer_Friendly_Version_Utility/1; Internet; accessed 12 January 2010.

[19] Ibid.

[20] Jonathan Leeman, "The Preemptive Resignation–A Get Out of Jail Free Card?" Web page; available from http://www.9marks.org/eJournal/preemptive - resig- nation-get-out-of-jail-free-card; Internet; accessed 11 August 2011.

[21] Ibid.

[22] Ibid.

[23] Mark Dever, op. Cit.

[24] Ibid.

[25] J.L. Dagg, *Manual of Church Order* (Harrisburg, VA: Gano Books, 1990), 274.

[26] Mark Dever, op. Cit.

Made in the USA
Monee, IL
15 November 2022

17839800R00085